PROFILES IN SPORTS COURAGE

PROFILES IN SPORTS COURAGE

KEN RAPPOPORT

Ω
PEACHTREE
ATLANTA

Ω

Published by
PEACHTREE PUBLISHERS
1700 Chattahoochee Avenue
Atlanta, Georgia 30318-2112

www.peachtree-online.com

Manufactured in United States of America

Book design by Melanie McMahon Ives
Photo research by Ana L. Parker

Photo credits: pp. 2, 13, 20, 27, 32, 37, 44, 49, 52, 61, 66, 73, 78, 85, 92, 101, 106, 109, 116, 121, 128, 133, 138, 145—Associated Press/World Wide Sports
Cover photos—Associated Press/World Wide Sports

10 9 8 7 6 5 4 3 2 1
First Edition

Library of Congress Cataloging-in-Publication Data

Rappoport, Ken.
 Profiles in sports courage / by Ken Rappoport.-- 1st ed.
  p. cm.
 ISBN 1-56145-368-4
 1. Athletes--Biography--Juvenile literature. I. Title.
 GV697.A1R326 2006
 796.092'2--dc22

                    2005029486

*For Griffin, Camryn, Kayla, Adina, and Shayna
as they go forth to their brave new world*

CONTENTS

INTRODUCTION

People have long admired outstanding athletes. From the time when the ancient Greeks celebrated physical skills by establishing the Olympic Games, we have looked to men and women with unusual speed, strength, or agility as models for the best that humans can achieve.

Our expectations have been high and sometimes our athletes have disappointed us. But a few individuals have awed us not only because they displayed superior athletic skills, but also because they exhibited a strength of character and a tenacity that seemed to defy logic and allowed them to overcome seemingly insurmountable obstacles. They all had intangible qualities that somehow kept them going when most other people would have given up. These athletes have taught us that there is no one definition of courage: it comes in all types, shapes, and sizes.

Courage can mean overcoming a life-threatening disease and returning to the arena with renewed determination.

Courage can mean challenging those who warn that a woman has no place on the highest peaks of the Himalayas and trudging on through the blinding snow.

PROFILES IN SPORTS COURAGE

Courage can mean stoically facing racial abuse and being willing to be the first to step forward in the fight to win respect for black athletes on the playing field.

The men and women athletes in this book are living proof that courage can empower us to find the best within ourselves and help us rise above anyone's expectations— sometimes even our own—to achieve the seemingly impossible. I invite you to read on and get to know these extraordinary people who in their own way defined the meaning of courage.

—K. R.

1
MUHAMMAD ALI
The Greatest

*T*he year: 1967

The place: the U.S. Army induction center in Houston, Texas

"Cassius Clay!" the military officer called out. "Army!"

No one came forward.

"Clay! Army!" he repeated.

Again, no response.

Cassius Clay refused to answer. He refused to step forward.

The officer approached. Did Clay know the penalty for his actions? Prison. A heavy fine.

Clay stood his ground. His face was a mask of determination. He was not, repeat, not going to serve in the Army.

Other young men had been busy all morning filling out forms and taking physical examinations. All of them were prepared to take the oath to defend their country.

All of them, that is, but the man they called Clay. This man who now answered to Muhammad Ali, his new Muslim name, had chosen a different path.

Call him Cassius Clay or Muhammad Ali, he was best known by only one identity: heavyweight boxing champion of the world.

Muhammad Ali carries the Olympic torch at the Centennial Games.

Why would a boxing champion refuse to defend his country?

Ali was now a minister of Islam. According to his religion, he did not have to serve in the armed forces. He had declared himself a conscientious objector, a person who refuses on moral or religious grounds to fight in a war.

Representatives of the Army tried to convince Ali to change his mind. They said he could put on exhibition fights for the troops and never go to battle.

Ali still refused. "I'd be just as guilty as the ones doing the killing," he said.

Cassius Clay had been a colorful, popular sports figure. But with his new name and his outspoken stand against the war and against the government, he became controversial.

Some people didn't accept Ali's claim to be a conscientious objector. They called Muhammad Ali another name: draft dodger. They thought he was a coward, using his new religion as an excuse not to fight in the Vietnam War.

Others took Ali's side. They admired him for standing up for his beliefs.

In 1964, he had won the heavyweight championship. And now, three years later, the self-proclaimed "Greatest" was preparing to fight a different kind of battle:

Ali vs. the U.S. government.

Cassius Marcellus Clay Jr. was born in Louisville, Kentucky, on January 17, 1942. His parents named him after a famous Kentucky abolitionist, a man who had devoted much of his career to fighting for the rights of blacks.

Clay grew up in a household where religion and hard work were highly valued. The prizefighter recalled that as a young boy he and his family lived in "semi-poverty." They lived in a four-room frame house that constantly needed fixing, but there was rarely enough money for repairs. More often, the family income went to basic necessities like food and clothing. Clay and his brother Rudy usually wore second-hand clothes.

The prizefighter's father Cassius Marcellus Clay Sr. worked as a sign painter, and his mother Odessa worked as a domestic. When he was old enough, young Clay found a job as a part-time janitor. Proud of their son, the Clays saved enough to buy him a bicycle when he was twelve. He was thrilled with his new bike. He rode it everywhere.

Then something happened that changed his life. While Clay was attending a bazaar at a community center, his bicycle disappeared. Stolen.

Searching for a policeman, Clay was directed to the basement of the community center. There a police officer named Joe Martin was teaching a boxing class.

The grief-stricken Clay reported the theft to the cop and told him he wanted to get even with the person who stole his bike. Martin advised Clay to learn to defend himself and invited the young man into his class. Clay agreed, and soon he was devoting most of his spare time to boxing. In addition to the lessons, he began training with a man named Fred Stoner at a gym in an all-black section of Louisville. Noticing Clay was a quick learner, Stoner helped him develop a distinctive boxing style.

Clay went at the sport with an almost scientific precision. He trained day in and day out, quite often alone, until his arms and legs were incredibly strong. He learned to stay in constant motion, bobbing his head and shifting his feet. Participating in dozens of amateur bouts, he began to perfect his skills. With his marvelous head fakes and fast foot movements, he could jab his opponent again and again without fear of being hit back. Most of the time, he walked away from a fight without a scratch.

Soon he developed what he called "built-in radar." He instinctively knew when to jab, when to move back, when to duck, and when to tie his man up.

Clay's aggressive personality was immediately obvious to Martin. He was "sassy…a little smart aleck," Martin said, but "he had more determination than most boys, and he had the speed to get him someplace."

Martin set him up with regular appearances on "Tomorrow's Champions," a local TV boxing show. Talkative and cocky, Clay became a popular guest on the program.

As Clay continued to win bout after bout on "Tomorrow's Champions," his confidence grew. He bragged about his strength. He felt he was invincible and said that no one could beat him. Not even much heavier, bigger opponents.

In July 1958, a sixteen-year-old Clay climbed into the ring against Charley Baker, a huge and muscular opponent who outweighed him by 23 pounds. Clay was a light heavyweight, and Baker a heavyweight.

Clay was forewarned by one friend, "You're crazy if you ever get in the ring with him."

Clay's response: "I'm gonna whip him."

He did—winning a unanimous three-round decision.

One day three young boxers entered the gym when Clay was training. Because he was training by himself, they thought Clay was an easy mark.

"You can take him," said one of the men to his young boxer friend.

At the next week's telecast, the young boxer climbed into the ring against Clay. Next thing he knew, he was flat on his back. Clay had knocked him unconscious.

The defeated boxer's friends couldn't believe it. It was only later they found out the Clay kid trained by himself because no one would get in the ring with him.

Clay did not disappoint his trainers. In fact, he rarely lost a fight.

By the time he was eighteen, he had fought all over the U.S. and had beaten just about every opponent. He won several Golden Gloves championships and two national AAU titles, but he was proudest when he became an Olympic boxing champion.

The gold medal thrilled Clay. He wore it around his neck all the time. Then an incident in a restaurant put a completely different light on all his achievements.

During a victorious trip back home to Louisville, Clay proudly displayed the medal he had won at the Rome Olympics. When he walked into an all-white restaurant in Louisville, the owner refused to admit a black man. The gold medal didn't mean anything to him. It didn't matter that Clay was an Olympic champion. Clay realized that people in Louisville still treated blacks like inferiors, no matter how impressive their accomplishments.

He was furious.

"There were places I couldn't go, places I couldn't eat [in]," the young boxer said.

Later that night Clay ran into trouble again. The leader of a white motorcycle gang demanded that Clay turn over his medal. A fight broke out. Although Clay escaped serious injury, he felt depressed and disillusioned. He hated the unfair treatment of blacks in America. Walking along the Ohio River, Clay was so upset he threw his prized Olympic medal right into the river!

He was angry and discouraged, but he had no plans to quit.

Next stop for Clay: the pros. He started making a name for himself. He was as quick with his mouth as he was with his fists. Crowds came to see this boastful kid fight, and fans eagerly read his cocky quotes in the sports section of the newspapers. Before long he earned the nicknames "The Louisville Lip" and "Motor Mouth."

Clay always predicted victory for himself. He was as good as his word. Nineteen opponents up, nineteen down. With this shining record, Clay earned a shot at Sonny Liston's heavyweight crown.

Two black fighters battling for the heavyweight title was no longer a novelty. Earlier in the twentieth century black fighters were in the minority, and black champions even more rare. Many good black fighters were denied the chance to step into the ring for a championship bout because of skin color.

Jack Johnson was the first African American to win the heavyweight championship in 1908. Because he was black and because many people considered him arrogant, he was not popular with most white boxing fans.

American society did not fully accept blacks as boxing champions until the 1930s, when Joe Louis wore the heavyweight crown.

By the time Louis became champion, he had won over many white fans. They not only appreciated his great boxing skills, but his humble manner. In their minds, Louis was an acceptable role model for all blacks.

Clay was anything but humble. He was convinced that he could defeat Liston, and he didn't mind saying so. But he wasn't given much of a chance against the champ. Only three of forty-three sports writers picked Clay to beat Liston in the fight in Miami Beach, Florida, on February 25, 1964. The general thinking: the veteran Liston was older, wiser, and tougher—entirely too tough for Clay.

Liston was a formidable opponent. He made appearances wearing a robe with the hood pulled up. His trainer called it "an executioner's robe." One commentator said, "He is the most frightening man in the world."

Billy Conn, the former light heavyweight champion, said, "He [Clay] hasn't the experience. The only experience he'll get with Liston is how to get killed in a hurry."

Because the *New York Times* thought the fight would be so one-sided, the newspaper didn't send its regular boxing correspondent. Instead, the *Times* assigned a reporter to a nearby hospital, certain that Clay would wind up there after the fight.

Clay, meanwhile, was pulling all sorts of stunts to promote himself. He could even manage to turn a potential disaster into an opportunity for favorable press coverage.

Around the time of the championship bout, the Beatles were on their first American tour. The famed musical group from England was expecting to be photographed with Liston, the champ, for a publicity shot. Instead, the Beatles got the champ's challenger. They were angry. And to make them even more furious, Clay was late. "Let's get the hell out of here," said John Lennon, and the Beatles started for the door.

Clay's press agent reacted quickly, and the police blocked the Beatles' escape. The Fab Four were not amused. After several minutes, Clay finally burst into the room.

"Hello there, Beatles," Clay said. "We oughta do some road shows together. We'll get rich."

Even the Beatles couldn't resist the charm of the Louisville Lip. The five of them went into the ring. Clay threw a mock punch. The Beatles pretended to go down like dominoes. Everybody was laughing. The photo made the front pages around the world.

Everything was about to change—for the Beatles and for Clay.

The fight was a matchup of different styles. There was nothing fancy about Liston. He was a brutal slugger who wore other boxers down with brute force. Liston would stand toe to toe with his opponent, and the last man standing was the winner. Usually, that was Liston.

Clay was the exact opposite. He moved around the ring on quick feet, jabbing quickly, then dancing away from his adversary's fists. His hit-and-run routine often had opponents reeling. Even so, few thought that Clay could last the entire fifteen rounds against such a deadly puncher as Liston—a grim-faced fighter Clay had called a "monster."

But Clay had a plan.

In the months leading up to the fight, Clay was a trash-talking terror.

"Liston is a tramp! I'm the champ! I want that big, ugly bear!" Clay shouted after Liston had knocked out former champion Floyd Patterson for the second time.

One night Liston looked out the window of his Denver house to see a bus parked on his lawn. The bus, painted red and white, displayed a sign saying, "World's Most Colorful Fighter: Liston Must Go In Eight."

It was Clay.

Screaming like a maniac, Clay threatened to break down Liston's door. Reporters had a field day, and Clay got lots of publicity.

At the pre-fight weigh-in, "The Mouth That Roared" went into his act again. And what an act it was!

He looked insane. He lunged at Liston, shouting, "I'm the champ. I'm ready to rumble!" Clay had to be forcibly restrained from attacking his opponent.

Had Clay finally gone over the edge? Or was it just a carefully rehearsed show?

No matter how they looked at it, most people agreed it was a shocking performance. "Why don't you hush up," Liston growled at Clay, "so everybody won't know you're a fool." Liston referred to Clay as "crazy." Many onlookers agreed.

Clay offered a prediction for the fight: He would knock out Liston in the eighth round.

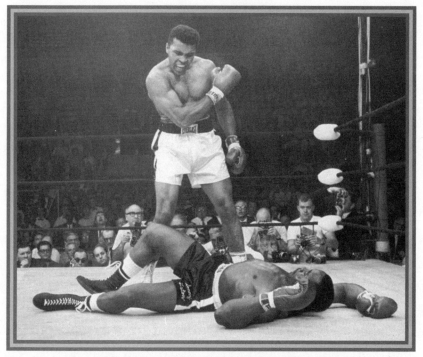

*Heavyweight champion Muhammad Ali stands over fallen challenger
Sonny Liston in a 1965 bout.*

When the referee brought the two together in the ring for
the pre-fight instructions, Liston glared at Clay to intimidate
him. Even though Clay had every reason to be scared, he
looked at the champion and said, "I've got you now, sucker!"

The bell rang. Clay whirled around the ring. He would
not let Liston get any clear shots at him. When they were in
close, Clay's head fakes kept him out of range from Liston's
deadly fists. Clay taunted his opponent. He cut him up with
savage punches. He danced away before Liston could con-
nect solidly.

He was supposed to kill me, thought Clay as he went to his corner. *Well, I'm still alive.* The longer Clay stayed in the ring, the more confident he became. Gradually he looked more and more like a champion and Liston looked very tired.

Float like a butterfly, sting like a bee.

This was an expression Clay would repeat over the years. It became a trademark expression describing his fighting style.

At the end of the fourth round, one of Clay's trainers noticed that something was wrong with the fighter. Clay was squinting and blinking. There was a terrible problem with his eyes!

In the corner between rounds, Clay was frantic.

"I can't see! Cut 'em off! I can't see! Cut off the gloves!"

His eyes were burning. Ointment from Liston's gloves had apparently rubbed off and irritated Clay's eyes. He wanted to quit. But his trainers wouldn't let him. They worked furiously, trying to wash the stinging ointment from the boxer's eyes. The bell rang for the fifth round.

Clay was like a gladiator suddenly stricken blind, but he went out to face Liston. If his adversary landed a solid blow, Clay knew he was finished. He struggled to stay out of Liston's way, trying to keep from being injured. He was hoping his tears would wash out his eyes. They still felt like they were being stuck by tiny needles.

"I could open them just enough to get a good glimpse of Liston," Clay said, "and then it hurt so bad, I blinked them closed again."

Muhammad Ali

By the sixth round, Clay's sight was restored. Bravely, he had turned tragedy to triumph. Now Clay's confidence soared. He peppered Liston with left-and-right combinations. The older fighter was faltering.

Liston was not able to get off his stool for the seventh round. Clay was the winner by a TKO (technical knockout)!

He was one round off his prediction, but close enough. Liston was a battered and beaten fighter. Clay was the new heavyweight champion of the world.

The gleeful Clay grabbed the broadcaster's microphone. "I'm champion of the world!" he roared. "I'm the greatest thing that ever lived.... I shook up the world! I shook up the world! I shook up the world!"

The day after the fight, Clay shook up America. He announced that he had become a Muslim and that he was dropping his "slave name." He was no longer Cassius Clay, but Cassius X. Within a short time he adopted the name Muhammad Ali, given to him by the leader of the Nation of Islam.

An incident Clay remembered from years earlier influenced his desire to join the black nationalist Nation of Islam. When Clay was twelve, he read about the murder of a young black boy about his age. Why was the boy killed? He had flirted with a white girl. An all-white jury decided in less than an hour to set the boy's white killers free. After the trial, one of the jurors said, "If we hadn't stopped to drink pop, it wouldn't have taken that long."

Clay was outraged at America's treatment of its black

citizens. No wonder he was attracted as an adult to a group that celebrated the superior virtues of blacks.

Clay's decision to unite with the Black Muslims drew harsh criticism. Many people associated the group with violence. By calling for separation from a corrupt white society, the Black Muslims challenged white America's view of itself and disturbed some black leaders.

"When Cassius joined the Black Muslims, he became a champion of racial segregation," said Martin Luther King Jr., "and that is what we were fighting against."

In 1965, Ali faced Liston again. This time he knocked him out in the first round. Ali successfully defended his title seven more times before his draft call from the Army in 1967.

After his refusal to be inducted into the armed forces, Ali was stripped of his heavyweight crown. His boxing license was taken away. He could no longer make millions of dollars in the ring.

The following summer a federal court convicted Ali of violating the Selective Service Act. He was fined $10,000 and sentenced to five years in jail.

Ali was freed on appeal, but he was no longer free to step into a ring. His boxing career was on hold, his future uncertain. Hard to believe, but the "Louisville Lip" was silenced—at least for the time being. The convictions had Ali reeling. But he was not one to sit on the sidelines for long.

While his case was being appealed to higher courts, Ali lectured at college campuses. He addressed Muslim meetings. He acted in a Broadway play.

Ali also spoke at peace rallies. At this time the Vietnam War had sharply divided America into two camps: the pro-war "Hawks" and the anti-war "Doves." Ali was the most visible figure for the "Doves." In the meantime, Ali's appeal went all the way to the top court in the country. As he waited for a decision from the Supreme Court, he thought about the decisions and sacrifices he had made since 1967. He had lost millions of dollars and some of the best years of his boxing career. That did not matter to Ali. He said, "My principles are more important than the money or my title."

During the summer of 1970, Ali bought an orange at a grocery store in Chicago and walked out the door. He heard shouts and turned around. The storekeeper was running toward him.

"You're free! You're free!" the man shouted. "The Supreme Court just said so."

The Supreme Court had just reversed the lower court's conviction of Ali. It had taken the courts three and a half years to decide the case. Four months later, a federal court ruled that Ali could box again. Muhammad Ali had chosen a cause over his boxing career. Now he was free to go back to the sport he loved.

In the next six years, Ali won two of the most famous fights in history. He knocked out heavyweight champion

George Foreman in the "Rumble in the Jungle" in Africa. He beat close rival Joe Frazier in the exhausting and memorable "Thrilla in Manila."

Before he retired in 1981, Ali became the first boxer to win the heavyweight title three times.

Muhammad Ali won decisions in the ring many times. But his biggest decision took place in a courtroom. He stood up for what he believed and won his case against the U.S. government.

That may have been Ali's most important victory of all.

2
LANCE ARMSTRONG
Captain Courageous

As he swung onto the seat of his bicycle, miracle man Lance Armstrong gazed at the steep mountain road ahead. Could he do it? Could he make sports history?

It was late in the 2003 Tour de France—a race Armstrong had ruled in recent years. A victory would give him five Tour de France championships, equaling the record of four other five-time winners.

Only Spain's Miguel Indurain had won five consecutive Tour titles. Armstrong hoped to match that, and would have loved nothing more than to win a record-breaking sixth in 2004.

But first he had to worry about the 2003 race. And there was some reason for concern.

Armstrong was struggling to hold onto his dwindling lead over Germany's Jan Ullrich as he prepared to brave the scary French Pyrenees Mountains. Armstrong led by a razor-thin 15 seconds, and this was a daunting place to try to increase his advantage over the other cyclists. Less than a week remained in the race. Could he win again?

"Lance is God." A fan held the sign high in the air as the cyclists rode by. But at the moment, Armstrong seemed all too human.

Overall leader Lance Armstrong rides past the Arc de Triomphe during the final stage of the 2000 Tour de France cycling race.

It had been four straight years of decisive victories for Armstrong in the Tour de France. But as he prepared to start the mountain ascent, the American racing star faced the biggest challenge of his career.

Now, go!

Armstrong, wearing the yellow jersey of the leader, bent forward. He started pedaling furiously. He climbed higher and higher up the steep, twisty mountain roads of the Pyrenees.

Armstrong was riding along smoothly when—

Look out!

Lance Armstrong

He didn't know what had hit him at first. Suddenly, there he was, sprawled flat on the asphalt. His bike had careened off to the side.

What had happened? An excited young fan waving a yellow tote bag had accidentally hooked Armstrong's handlebars and sent him flying. For the moment, the champion cyclist couldn't catch his breath.

With tremendous effort, Armstrong struggled back on his feet. Quickly, he surveyed the damage. He shook his head. The bike chain had snapped off. Angry and frustrated, he started to rethread the chain. Precious seconds were being lost. Under his breath he screamed every swear word he knew.

"It was one of the most intense feelings I've had in my life," Armstrong said. "Your back is against the ropes. They're coming at you, and you've been losing it all week, and now you're about to lose it all. What's your answer? What are you going to do?"

Why, get back on the bicycle, of course.

In a show of sportsmanship, his closest competitor Jan Ullrich slowed down with other riders until Armstrong and another fallen rider could remount and continue. Ullrich was repaying a similar courtesy from Armstrong when the German had fallen in a previous Tour de France race.

Hurting from his fall, angry and scared, Armstrong remounted his bike. In his haste, his right foot slipped off the pedal. Armstrong hurtled across the top of his bike onto the handlebars. He recovered quickly and pedaled furiously. His personal coach was watching on TV, and he saw the look on Armstrong's face.

PROFILES IN SPORTS COURAGE

All the world thought Armstrong was finished. His coach Chris Carmichael had a different viewpoint.

"This is going to be a good thing," he said. "Lance rides much better when he has some emotion."

Only one other person had won the punishing Tour de France five straight times. Could Armstrong match that incredible feat, and then come back the next year for a record sixth in a row?

Growing up in Plano, Texas, young Lance Armstrong loved competition.

"When it came to the [sports] with balls [like football] I wasn't very good," he said. "I was determined to be good at something, though. When I was in the fifth grade, my school had a running race. The night before, I told my mom I was going to be a champ."

Armstrong won the race. He never looked back.

At the age of thirteen, he joined the local swimming club. After one year he was one of the best swimmers in the state. His stamina, energy, and work habits astounded his team-mates and coaches. Armstrong was a human dynamo.

He would hop on his bike and ride six miles to get to swimming practice. He would swim for four hours, usually beating everybody in the pool. Then it was back on his bike for the long ride home.

Cocky and brash, Armstrong "talked trash" to his opponents. Whether swimming or biking or running cross-country on his school track team, Armstrong was openly confident he would win. More often than not, he was as good as his word.

Lance Armstrong

Armstrong loved to race. He traveled with friends far and wide to find competition good enough to meet his standards.

At age fourteen, he entered his first triathlon, a grueling event that combines bicycling, running, and swimming over long distances.

"I liked the endurance, the gritting-it-out part of triathlons," Armstrong said.

Without even training, Armstrong won the first triathlon he entered. He was a natural. One year later, he was a national junior triathlon champion. Still a teenager, he was soon beating adults in triathlon competition and earning $20,000 a year.

He was known for his fiery and free spirit. And no one was going to quell it, not even the coach of the U.S. national bicycle racing team.

In 1991, Armstrong participated as an amateur in an important international pro-am race in Italy. He was asked to slow down by the American coach so a popular professional rider on their team could win.

Slow down? Was the coach kidding?

Armstrong, always the determined competitor, sped up. He went on to win the race, even though angry fans tossed tacks on the roadway in an attempt to stop him.

The next year, Armstrong turned pro. He wanted to compete in bicycle races in Europe, where cycling was just as popular as baseball and football in America. In his very first race, the Classica San Sebastian in Spain, hardly anyone noticed him—except his teammates. Armstrong finished last in a field of 111, but that was not important to him.

"I was 30 minutes off the back and it was raining," Armstrong recalled. "It was raining so hard it hurt. But I had to finish. I didn't do it to impress anyone. Just to finish. That night, my teammates said they realized I wasn't normal."

With Armstrong's skills and unusual enthusiasm, it was just a matter of time before he would start winning consistently. In 1993 he gained the title of U.S. road racing champion. That same year, Armstrong won the world road-race title and established himself as a bicycle-racing superstar.

And along the way he had developed a unique racing style.

"I'm on the bike. I go into a rage," Armstrong said. "I shriek for about five seconds, I shake like mad, and my eyes kind of bulge, and I'd never quit.

"That's heart. That's soul. That's guts."

Armstrong had already won every major bike race in the United States and some in Europe. Next stop: Tour de France, the most famous and challenging bike race in the world. The timid need not apply. The Tour de France is a fierce endurance test. It covers more than 2,000 rugged miles through the mountains, valleys, and villages of France. Lining the route and filling the towns are millions of fans who have come to this part of France for the thrilling summer spectacle.

The race is run in "stages," with each day considered a separate stage. It takes about three weeks to finish. The racer with the fastest combined time in all the stages earns the traditional yellow jersey of the Tour de France winner.

Lance Armstrong

The race winds up in Paris. The winner receives a hero's welcome amidst roaring crowds as he rides his bicycle down the world-famous roadway, the Champs Elysées. He is accompanied by his "team"—a group of cyclists that performs various tasks to ease the way for the lead racer. They check the road ahead for problems. They map out racing strategy. They supply food and drink. They sometimes provide a "cocoon" to shield the main rider from the wind and other riders. No one wins the Tour de France alone.

Not long after winning the world road-race title, Armstrong won one of the stages of the Tour de France. Only twenty-five years old, he seemed to be on his way to greatness.

But suddenly his dreams of glory threatened to turn into a nightmare. In October 1996, Armstrong received the news. His most difficult battle was about to begin: his fight against cancer. The disease had reached an advanced stage. The doctors said it would take a miracle to beat it.

"You can't help but have feelings that you're not going to make it," Armstrong said.

But he was going to find some way to defeat this tough opponent. Armstrong had been a fighter all his life. He never considered giving up.

"I tried my best to treat cancer like I would a race," Armstrong said. "I was determined to win."

He felt that if he was well prepared and knowledgeable, he could handle anything. When the doctors told him he needed immediate surgery, he didn't hesitate. He made it through the operation, then underwent long, uncomfortable chemotherapy treatments.

Lance hated being sick. He hated feeling his body grow weaker and weaker. He had no intention of giving in to the weakness, though. He started cycling again.

Before his illness he could ride for hours. Now the smallest hills were a problem. He often felt like he was going to throw up. It was frustrating. But these were problems he could conquer. Even though he was weak and sick, he was out there on his bike.

Race again? Unthinkable.

Think again.

Remarkably, within a year Armstrong was pronounced cancer-free. The doctors, the surgery, and the chemo had done their jobs. Now Armstrong slowly worked himself back into shape. He'd made up his mind to race again.

And he did. He dropped out of some races because he was too weak, but he kept racing. Finally, success. In 1998, he wound up fourth in the Tour of Spain. Then he finished fourth at the world championships.

Getting back to the Tour de France was his major goal. But his biggest worry was conquering the tough mountain stages where the race is usually won or lost. Steep ascents had never been Armstrong's strong point. In four previous Tour de France starts, he had only managed to finish once—at a distant thirty-sixth place.

By 1999, though, he felt ready for the challenge. "Prior to getting sick," Armstrong said, "I was a little heavier, so climbing was a bit more difficult. When I recovered, I had lost some weight, so that made it a little bit easier to compete in the mountains."

He got off to a fast start that year with a record-breaking run in the time trials on the first day. He wiped out the mark of Spain's superstar Miguel Indurain.

Armstrong was back, and better than ever.

Lance Armstrong in 2005, after winning his seventh straight Tour de France cycling race

But what about the mountain climbs that had given him so much trouble before?

After taking the lead on the first day, Armstrong more than held his own on those treacherous mountain roads. Holding American flags high, Armstrong and his teammates entered Paris way ahead of the pack.

Crowds along the Champs Elysées greeted the new Tour de France champion.

Having beaten cancer, Armstrong had pulled off another

miracle. He had won his first Tour de France title! And he had done it in record time—an average speed of 25 miles per hour over the 2,285-mile course.

"I'm in shock, I'm in shock, I'm in shock," Armstrong repeated. "It was a long road to get to the Tour, and a longer one to get through it."

How could Armstrong top that? How about another Tour de France title in 2000? One more in 2001? And still another in 2002? Armstrong dominated every race, winning by wide margins. His fourth title eclipsed the American record of Greg Lemond, the first cyclist from the U.S. to capture the Tour de France since it began in 1903. Lemond won in 1986, 1989, and 1990.

But now it was 2003, and Armstrong's position as reigning Tour champion looked shaky. He was the weakest he had ever been, thanks to a bout with the flu. He had hip tendonitis. And a mass pileup during the first stage had left him with a tire mark on his back and feeling a bit wobbly.

As the race entered into its second week, Armstrong was clinging to a thin lead. But everyone could see that he was struggling.

"He was tired," said David Millar, a cyclist from England. "He was having to push himself, which was maybe not a new experience for Lance, but was a new experience for the rest of us to see. It gave everyone hope."

Armstrong had further weakened when he had run out of water during a time trial in sizzling 104-degree weather. He'd arrived at the end of his run up the mountain parched and dehydrated.

"I had an incredible crisis," he said. "At one point I felt I was pedaling backward. It's the most thirsty I've been in a time trial."

Armstrong had lost almost nine pounds. He had also lost 96 seconds of his lead to Ullrich, the German cyclist who had won the Tour de France in 1997. Now only 34 seconds separated the two racers.

Armstrong was dispirited.

"That's as close as I've come to just getting off the bike and quitting," he said.

Then Armstrong's lead was cut to merely 15 seconds following the next day's stage in the Pyrenees Mountains. He looked puzzled and dejected.

"It's obvious I'm not riding as well as in years past, and I don't know why," he said. "Something's not clicking."

The next day Armstrong was determined to break away. He started with a strong sprint up the mountains, only to be slowed down by the careless spectator's tote bag. After his sprawl on the asphalt, Armstrong had to continue on a bike with a cracked rear chain stay.

Suddenly Armstrong felt a "big, big rush of adrenaline." He climbed back on his bike and started pedaling furiously up the mountain road.

"I was desperate," Armstrong said.

The look of determination on Armstrong's face was unmistakable.

"I saw the same thing when he was fighting cancer," said Armstrong's coach. "The same fortitude. The same intensity. It was eerie."

With that "rush of adrenaline," Armstrong reclaimed the race. He finished with his fifth straight Tour de France victory—tying the records of five-time winners Jacques Anquetil (1957, '61 through '64); Eddy Merckx ('69 through '72, '74); Bernard Hinault ('78, '79, '81, '82, '85); and Miguel Indurain ('91 through '95). Armstrong also tied Indurain's mark of consecutive victories.

Then, in 2004, he broke the record with number six.

Why stop at six? Remarkably, Armstrong added number seven in 2005!

It was an awesome achievement—seven straight Tour de France victories simply defied imagination.

More importantly, Armstrong had shown the courage of a champion by making the most of a second chance.

3
KERRI STRUG
Standing Tall

*I*t was the 1996 Summer Olympics in Atlanta. The American female gymnasts known as the "Magnificent Seven" were getting ready for their final vault.

In previous years, the Russians and Romanians had dominated the gymnastic competition. This time, the Americans were battling the Russians for the gold medal.

And what a battle it had been. The Russians led the first day. The next day the Americans passed them with an awesome display on the uneven bars. The Americans kept the lead with brilliant work on the balance beam and a magnificent show on the floor routines. The crowd at the Georgia Dome in Atlanta filled the arena with their cheers.

All the Americans needed for the gold medal was a strong performance in the vault competition.

Kerri Strug had watched as her teammates made their jumps.

Next up was Dominique Moceanu, the American star who usually excelled at the vault.

She fell. Then she fell again.

"I saw Dom fall the first time," Strug said, "and I thought, I

Kerri Strug performs during the 1996 Summer Olympic Games.

can't believe it. Then she fell a second time and it was like time stopped."

Strug knew the Russians were doing their floor exercises. She also knew it could be a high scoring event. "My heart was beating like crazy."

The medal looked as if it was slipping from the Americans' grasp.

It would be up to Strug. One good vault from the eighteen-year-old would cinch the gold medal. The vault was one of Strug's best events. She hadn't missed a perfect landing in practice or competition for three months.

"She is the one who can do it anytime, anywhere," her coach Bela Karolyi had said.

Strug was confident, too. That's why she was so surprised by what happened.

On her first vault she flipped and fell hard on her left ankle. She heard a "snap" and found herself sprawled on the ground.

"My first thought was," she later reported, "'How could you do that?'"

When she tried standing, violent pain shot through her ankle. The pain worried her, but there was another problem.

"I can't feel my leg!" she shouted to Karolyi. "It's numb."

"Numb?" Karolyi asked. "What do you mean, numb?"

"Numb," Strug said with a gasp. "I can't feel a thing."

Strug had another jump coming—if she was able to jump, that is.

"There's something wrong with me," Strug repeated to herself. Then she said a little prayer. "Please, Lord, help me out here."

The petite gymnast hesitated for a moment. She hobbled around on the sidelines, barely able to walk. The Olympic gold medal was within reach for the U.S. team. So much depended on her.

"You can do it, Kerri," Karolyi said. "You can do it."

She had thirty seconds to decide if she could jump. The pain in her ankle was almost unbearable.

It seemed that Kerri Strug had been practicing for this moment all her life. As a toddler she loved tumbling around the living room of her home in Tucson, Arizona. It didn't please her father, Burt, a heart surgeon. He kept asking his

daughter to "please walk on your feet. You're always traveling upside-down."

Kerri's older sister Lisa was a gymnast. Like most young
girls, Kerri wanted to be just like her big sister. At the age of
six, Kerri was getting lessons from the gymnastics coach at
the University of Arizona.

"I saw how in college everything was team oriented,"
Kerri said, "and everyone had a lot of fun. That was my goal
before I ever competed in the Olympics."

She was only twelve years old when she decided to leave
home. She wanted to go to Houston to train with Bela Karolyi,
one of the foremost gymnastics teachers in the world.

"I was devastated," Kerri's mother said.

Leaving her family behind was just as tough for Kerri.
But she had a dream. She wanted to be the next Mary Lou
Retton or Nadia Comaneci. They were two of Karolyi's most
famous gymnasts. Even at twelve, Kerri was already thinking about Olympic glory.

"I knew if I was going to make the '92 [Olympic] team, I
would have to make a change," Kerri said.

In Houston, Kerri moved in with a family close to
Karolyi's gym. The Romanian-born coach was as famous as
the gymnasts he turned out. He had a reputation for being
tough—extremely tough. And he lived up to it.

"It was very hard at times," Kerri said. "When you got
down or had a bad day, you got to a phone and talked to
your parents a lot."

When school was out, the gymnasts trained in a secluded

camp an hour away from Houston. Kerri shared a log cabin with Dominique Moceanu. The gymnasium was nearby.

Training was difficult. All the gymnasts worked out six to seven days a week, eight hours a day. Kerri didn't have much time to be homesick. Generally, it was just work, eat, and sleep—when she could.

"Her basic personality was not that aggressive," Karolyi said of Strug. "I always had to handle her like a baby. That's what we called her, the 'Baby', because she was always the youngest."

Kerri tried out for the 1992 U.S. Olympic team. On the last day of the trials, everything was going smoothly for her. Then during her routine in the floor exercise, she fell.

Kerri felt she had lost the chance of a lifetime. But in spite of the fall, her overall showing was good. The "Baby" had made the U.S. Olympic team at the age of fourteen.

She was the youngest U.S. athlete at the Games in Barcelona, Spain. The American girls came home with the bronze medal in the team competition.

A team medal, yes. But not the one that Kerri really wanted. She had dreamed of a medal in the individual competition. She didn't make it. A major disappointment. But she was determined to keep trying.

Suddenly, Kerri's world was turned upside down. Karolyi unexpectedly retired. For the next three years, Kerri drifted from coach to coach and gym to gym. She suffered a number of injuries. "They were the worst years of my life," she said.

Kerri wouldn't quit. She still had visions of competing in the 1996 Olympics in Atlanta. In August 1994, Kerri entered a minor gymnastics meet.

Climbing onto the uneven parallel bars, she suddenly lost her grip. She fell over backwards and tumbled to the mat. Her lower back was badly injured.

"That really scared my dad," she said. "An arm, a leg, it heals. But a back is different."

Doctors were not certain that Kerri would ever walk again, but this stubborn gymnast would not quit. Her recovery took six months, then it was back on the beam. She had put so much time and effort into gymnastics, she didn't want to walk away from the sport.

Good news: Karolyi decided to come out of retirement. Kerri had her old coach back, and new confidence. When she won the American Cup title in 1996, her confidence grew even more.

The gymnast, now eighteen, had achieved her first individual major championship. Kerri was excited. She had battled through injury and several coaching changes to make her mark on a great international stage. She felt good about herself, about her suddenly revived gymnastics career. Only 4-foot-9 and 78 pounds, Kerri was suddenly standing very tall.

Karolyi was impressed.

"I think pride made her come out of her shell this year," Karolyi said of Strug. "And since the American Cup, where she tasted the satisfaction of individual performance, she was like a totally new person."

Kerri Strug

Kerri Strug is carried by her coach, Bela Karolyi, to receive her gold medal at the 1996 Summer Olympic Games.

Next stop: the Olympics. Strug was now part of a group of experienced and accomplished teenagers that included Shannon Miller, Dominique Dawes, Dominique Moceanu, Amy Chow, Amanda Borden, and Jaycie Phelps. There were three former or current national champions on the team, and three of them were veterans of the 1992 Olympics.

Someone came up with a nickname for the American team: the "Magnificent Seven." The name came from a popular movie about a posse of tough gunslingers in the Old West. It was a remake of a Japanese classic called *The Seven Samurai*, a film about ancient warriors.

PROFILES IN SPORTS COURAGE

Like the original "Magnficent Seven," the U.S. gymnasts were bold, determined, and courageous. But the word "magnificent" also referred to their great talent.

This cool label suited the team. The enthusiastic American gymnasts wore snazzy "Mag 7" logos on their red, white, and blue uniforms. Kerri was proud just to be a part of such an outstanding group. But when she saw the starting lineup for the gymnastics event, she was surprised and a little uncertain.

In earlier competitions Strug had generally been over-shadowed by her teammates. "I was always second fiddle," she said. "If they took two girls to the finals [of an event] I was third. If they took three, I was fourth." But this time Karolyi had actually named her to lead off on the uneven bars, one of her worst events!

That wasn't the only surprise. Kerri would also go first on the dangerous and daunting balance beam. And she was tapped to "anchor" the team in both the floor exercises and the vault. The anchor gymnast has the most important role: to finish up the event and to clinch the victory.

"I know they're trying to take advantage of my [Barcelona Olympics] experience," Kerri said, "but I don't think anyone likes to have that much pressure on them."

No need to worry. In the Olympic medal competition, Kerri and her teammates were in top form. The Americans seemed to be having fun—until the vault.

After her fateful fall, Kerri had to decide what to do.

"Do I have to do the second vault?" she asked Karolyi.

Karolyi was not sure that the Americans at that point were safely ahead for the gold.

"I encouraged her," Karolyi said later, "but she was the one who had to answer that."

Kerri hopped around, trying not to put any stress on her injured foot. She knew that her ankle might very well be broken. Could she take a chance and go for another vault?

The judges, meanwhile, were scoring her first jump. She only had 30 seconds to prepare for the second.

Strug tried to push away the many memories of failures in important, pressure-packed situations. In the gymnastics world, some people had called her "Scary Kerri" behind her back for uneven performances though the years.

All eyes in the Georgia Dome were on Strug as she tried to shake off the injury.

"I could see she was hurt," said her mother Melanie. "As a parent, I'd have said, 'Don't do the vault.' But knowing Kerri, you couldn't have stopped her unless you'd dragged her off."

The seconds were ticking off. Kerri had to decide.

She thought: *This is it, Kerri. You've done this vault a thousand times.*

True, she told herself. *But not with a foot that was so badly injured you needed immediate medical attention.*

Although she was aware that an ambulance stood ready just outside the Georgia Dome, Kerri wasn't thinking about going to the hospital at the moment.

All she could think about was making her second vault a good one.

Kerri knew she could hurt herself so badly that she would not be able to compete in the individual competition. That didn't matter now. She put the team first.

"Everyone else had put so much time and sacrifice into it," Kerri said, thinking of her coach and her teammates. "I couldn't give up."

Kerri walked confidently back onto the runway. Even the slightest limp in her approach would affect her score.

"I let the adrenaline take over," she said.

Kerri was focused. She was thinking about the vault and nothing else.

Her approach was perfect. She raced down the runway and soared over the vaulting horse. She landed squarely on her feet.

"I felt pretty good in the air," she said, "but I felt good the time before, too. Then when I landed, I heard another crack."

She held the landing until the judges gave her the all-clear sign. Then she collapsed in agony.

"I felt like a bomb went off," Kerri said.

The Georgia Dome exploded with cheers and applause. The thrilled fans slapped each other on the back, exchanging high fives and hugging.

Medics rushed to Kerri's side. The scoreboard flashed her score of 9.7, wrapping up the gold medal for the United States.

Kerri Strug

She was placed on a stretcher. Kerri's parents wanted her to go right to the hospital. She wanted her gold medal. The music for the medal ceremony began and Kerri's teammates were waiting. "Bela, Bela," Strug cried, "they're taking me to the hospital."

"No one's taking you anywhere until you get your gold medal," the coach said.

With that he picked her up off the stretcher.

"Wave to the crowd, Kerri," he said.

She did as he carried her to the podium. The picture of Kerri in her coach's arms was front page all over America. So was this: the photo of Kerri standing on one leg for the "The Star-Spangled Banner," propped up by her teammates.

The gold medal belonged to the Americans. Only later did they find out Kerri's second jump wasn't needed. They had already earned enough points to beat the Russians.

Doctors said they had no idea how she had made her second jump. Kerri had a fractured left ankle, the kind of injury that would usually sideline an athlete for weeks.

Kerri had refused to let doctors cut off her vaulting shoes. She thought she could still use them in the individual competitions. Her second jump had ruined her chance for that. She was crushed about missing that opportunity. The individual championship was a lifelong dream.

But with her vault in the team competition, Kerri had already realized something far more special—more than she could know at the moment. With that courageous jump, she had defined the true ideal of the Olympic spirit.

Asked if anyone would remember her moment in the sun, Strug replied: "I think everyone realizes it took a lot of guts to go for it."

She was right. Millions of viewers will always remember the sight of that tiny gymnast, standing so tall.

4
JUNKO TABEI
No Mountain Too High

*J*unko Tabei opened her eyes wide when she heard the distant noise. Could it be thunder? The dull roar was getting louder and louder.

It was just after midnight on May 4, 1975. Junko and fourteen other mountain climbers had been asleep at their bone-chilling, windswept camp high up on Mount Everest.

The all-female group had reached Camp II, one of the stops the climbers use to rest and adapt themselves to the high altitude. Many others had reached the peak of the great mountain that straddled the Nepal-China border. They were all men. If she succeeded, Junko would be the first woman to climb the peak.

It was literally the biggest challenge of Junko's life. She had conquered many mountains, but never one like this. At 29,035 feet, Everest is generally considered the world's tallest peak.

Junko raised her head and listened intently to the growing rumble. It was not thunder. This dreaded sound could only mean one thing:

AVALANCHE!

Junko was terrified. She knew that in minutes a landslide of snow and ice would tear through their camp like a runaway train.

PROFILES IN SPORTS COURAGE

Junko Tabei in Tokyo, 1991

It would wipe out everything in sight.

The mountain climbers had very little time to think as the avalanche bore down on them in all its terrible fury. When it struck the camp, Junko and her companions were tossed around like sticks in a storm. They crashed into equipment. They smashed into each other. Then everything was quiet.

Junko found herself trapped under four bodies. She was buried alive under tons of snow. Her last thoughts were of her beautiful two-year-old daughter, Noriko. How she wished to see her again. Then she fell into unconsciousness...

Junko Ishibashi discovered her passion for mountain climbing quite by accident. She was only ten years old when she went along on a class trip to climb two modest-size peaks in Japan. The pace, she found, suited her gentle personality, and the mountains satisfied her love of adventure.

Junko enjoyed mountain climbing because it wasn't a competition. "Even if you go slow," she explained, "you can make it to the top. Or, if you must, you can quit in the middle."

Mountain climbing might have been a love for Junko, but not for her family. She and her six brothers and sisters lived in the small town of Miharumachi in northern Japan. The country was very poor following the Second World War.

"I couldn't think about climbing mountains, or any kind of leisure," she said. "We had to worry about what we would eat."

Still, Junko dreamed of climbing mountains.

Mountain climbers come in all shapes and sizes. But no one would have thought that the frail-looking Junko could ever conquer these tall and windswept peaks. "I was stamped as a weak child," Junko said. Even as an adult, Junko only grew to the height of 4-foot-9. She didn't seem hardy enough to be a successful mountain climber.

Her petite size wasn't her only handicap. When Junko was a young girl, most people thought that women were not meant to climb mountains. Women could not do it. Women *should* not do it. Climbing mountains was for men.

"In the 1970s in Japanese culture, the status of women was much lower than it is now," Junko said in a 2003 interview. "Usually, people think a woman should be at home looking after the children."

After finishing high school, Junko went to college to earn a teaching degree in English Literature. But she never forgot her first love. After graduation in 1962, she got back to mountain climbing in a big way. She joined several clubs that were primarily for men. Junko had a tough time being accepted.

"Some of the men wouldn't climb with me, but a few older ones were supportive," Junko said. "Some thought I was there to meet men," she added, "but I was only interested in climbing."

And climb she did! It didn't take long before she had scaled all of Japan's tallest peaks, including the world-famous Mt. Fuji. She earned money to pay for her climbs by working as a magazine editor.

In 1965, Junko married Masanobo Tabei, a well-known Japanese climber. In 1969, Junko formed the Joshi-Tohan (Women's Mountaineering) Club. It was the first of its kind in Japan.

"Mountains are not restricted to men only," Junko said.

Indeed. Only a year later Junko and her fellow female adventurers traveled to Nepal to tackle Annapurna III, one of the world's tallest mountains. It was the first climbing experience for Junko outside of Japan. After reaching the top of the 24,786-foot mountain, Junko turned her thoughts to climbing Mt. Everest.

She found opposition. "Some people really tried to stop me," she said, "but I knew I could do it."

Junko had problems finding money to pay for the expedition. It is very expensive to climb a mountain like Everest. Japanese companies were not eager to sponsor a mountain climbers club, particularly an *all-female* club.

Junko Tabei

"Most companies' reaction was that it's impossible for women to climb Mt. Everest," she said.

Getting a permit to climb the mountain was another problem. Restrictions were very tight. Anyone climbing Everest had to be approved by the Nepal government.

Junko knew it would be a long wait for approval. And it was—four years. Finally, at the age of thirty-five, she received the cherished permit. By that time, she had also found sponsors for the expedition.

Junko was sharply criticized in her own country. People felt she was neglecting her family. She was leaving her child and husband at home to pursue a dream. But to Junko this was no ordinary dream. In her mind Mt. Everest was a "holy ground" and a "place of the gods" in the Himalayas.

Besides, she was too fiercely independent to worry about what people thought. "If people want to call me 'that crazy mountain woman,' that's okay," she said.

So she led a fifteen-woman expedition on the greatest adventure of their lives. Five of them were married, including Junko. Several Nepalese Sherpas—people who make their living guiding visitors up the difficult slopes of the Himalayan mountains—completed the group.

The women knew it would not be easy. With the ever-present threat of avalanches, powerful winds, and subfreezing temperatures, Mt. Everest was a daunting challenge. Even more daunting: the incredible size of the mountain. There was no other mountain like it in the world.

Climbers of Mt. Everest usually stop at a base camp first and then four other camps on the way to the summit.

The women reached the base camp at 17,600 feet, and then Camp I at 19,500 before moving up to Camp II at 21,326. Everything was going according to plan—until the avalanche roared down and engulfed the entire party.

When Junko regained consciousness, her Sherpa guide was pulling her out of the snow by her ankles. He gave her oxygen to help her breathe. She ached from head to toe. Her body was covered with bruises. Worse, she had wrenched her back and could not walk.

But Junko was not defeated. "As soon as I knew every-one was alive," she said, "I was determined to continue."

It took two days for her to get back on her feet. Even then, she was wobbly and weak. A doctor traveling with the group feared for the climbers' safety. He recommended that they go back down the mountain. Forget about the rest of the climb.

Giving up was not in Junko's plans. She and her companions knew how far they had already come. "We were united," Junko said. They would not stop until they had reached the top of Everest.

Junko was barely able to walk, but she refused to give up her place at the head of the line. Crawling on her hands and knees at times, she led the group of women slowly and painfully up the perilous mountain slope.

Twelve days later, a battered and bruised Junko Tabei clawed her way to the top of Everest—the first woman to

Junko Tabei

Junko Tabei becomes the first woman to reach the top of Mt. Everest on May 16, 1975.

perform that feat! But her pain and exhaustion would not let her rejoice.

"All I felt was relief," she said.

Junko didn't fully appreciate the impact she had made until some time after the climb. By then she was well on her way to becoming an international celebrity.

She was decorated by the king of Nepal. He could only shake his head. He told Junko he was surprised that an all-woman team could climb so high. In her homeland she was invited to make speaking appearances. Her name was soon on the lips of most every Japanese citizen and appeared in books, in magazines, and on TV. The woman who had defied convention in Japan was now being honored by the Japanese government and held up as a role model.

Uncomfortable with her celebrity as the first woman to climb Everest, Junko played down her achievement. "I was the thirty-sixth person to climb Everest," she said modestly.

In time she would climb the highest mountain on each of the seven continents. Another first for a woman.

Of all the mountains she climbed, Junko felt a special attachment to Everest. While still climbing well into her sixties, she made time to help preserve the environment of the world's tallest peak.

Summing up her mountain climbing career in a 2003 interview, the sixty-three-year-old mother of two put it this way: "I like meeting unknown challenges."

Climbing Mt. Everest would certainly qualify.

5
JUNIUS KELLOGG
Blowing the Whistle

The waiting game began. The trap was set and Junius Kellogg was the bait.

This was a game Kellogg had never played, one involving gangsters and gamblers. As the star center for the Jaspers, the Manhattan College basketball team, he was used to a game of scoring points and grabbing rebounds.

He was still playing center, but in an entirely different arena. Kellogg was now the star of a cloak-and-dagger story as scary as any Hollywood movie thriller. Only this story was real, and so was the threat to Kellogg's life.

It had started with a knock on Kellogg's dormitory door on January 11, 1951. Standing before Kellogg was none other than Hank Poppe, Manhattan's co-captain from the season before.

Poppe was the last person Kellogg expected to see at his door. "This guy would pass me on the street and not even say so much as a good morning," Kellogg later remembered. The word was that Poppe hadn't been at all pleased when Kellogg became the first black player on the Manhattan team. So why was he at Kellogg's door? And why was he being so friendly?

Manhattan College center Junius Kellogg

Once he was inside Kellogg's dorm room, Poppe announced that he had a deal for Kellogg. He said he was going to make him rich.

The encounter between the two men went something like this:

"Junius, are you a gambler?" Kellogg glared. The visitor continued. "You know, there's lots of money to be made. I've got a proposition for you."

The visitor seemed unconcerned with the look of alarm spreading across Kellogg's face.

"You could make a thousand dollars if you're smart. If you throw the DePaul game on Tuesday..."

Poppe didn't get a chance to continue.

"Get out! Get out right now!" Kellogg screamed. "I don't want to hear any gambling talk!"

Junius Kellogg

Poppe backed toward the door, talking as he went.

"Look, it wouldn't hurt to listen, Junius. Think it over. I'll be in touch with you by 7:30 Sunday night by telephone."

Kellogg slammed the door after his unwelcome guest. He was so angry, he looked for something to throw, kick, or break. Then he realized what he had to do. Kellogg stormed out of the dormitory and went to find Manhattan College basketball coach Ken Norton…

Back in high school in Portsmouth, Virginia, Junius Kellogg was regarded as a "gentle giant" by his classmates. Gentle, and thoroughly honest.

He had long ago learned the value of honesty. His mother Lucy had made telling the truth one of the cardinal rules of the Kellogg household. The teachers at I. C. Norcom High School, a mostly black school, had continued to reinforce the importance of being honest.

Kellogg and his ten brothers and sisters had also learned the value of hard work. They didn't have to look any further than their own family. Their father, Theodore, was a laborer. Their mother also brought in money by cleaning other people's houses.

Junius was a member of the earliest basketball teams at Norcom High at a time when there was little money for sports. The players sold five-cent candy bars to raise money for uniforms.

There was no basketball court. The team played its

games outside, even in the bitter cold of winter, on the school's cinder track. "It was from that beginning that Norcom began to build a rich history in basketball," remembered James Holley, one of Kellogg's teammates.

Holley described Kellogg as easy-going. On a basketball court, though, he was anything but laid back. Kellogg was a big man, with talent and muscle to spare. He used his height to dominate a game.

After high school, Kellogg served in the U.S. Army and rose to the rank of sergeant. He played almost every sport available: basketball, football, and softball, in addition to boxing and joining the swimming team. One year, he was selected as the outstanding athlete for the entire Army!

In 1949, the people in the athletic department at Manhattan College were looking for new players with outstanding basketball skills. Kellogg caught their attention. He was 6-foot-10, an unusually tall player for that time. In those days, massive seven-footers like the players running around today's courts were rare.

Kellogg joined the Jaspers and immediately established them as one of the top teams in New York at a time when the "City Game" was as good as any in the country. He usually was the Jaspers' top scorer and with his imposing height, a powerful rebounder. One New York newspaper described Kellogg as a "sophomore ace" after he scored twenty-three points in an 87–57 victory over Dartmouth in the 1950–51 season.

Everything was going smoothly for Kellogg—until his

troubling encounter with Poppe in his dorm room in January. After that, Kellogg headed straight for Manhattan basketball coach Ken Norton. He approached Norton shortly before the Jaspers were to leave for a game against St. Peter's in Jersey City.

"Could I see you for a minute, Coach?"

Norton was not prepared for what he was about to hear.

"I have some shocking news for you," Kellogg said. "I've been offered a thousand dollars to see that we lose the DePaul game."

At first Norton was speechless. Then he asked, "Junie, did you tell anybody else about this?"

"No."

"Alright, keep your mouth shut. Don't mention it to anybody."

There was a pause, then Norton asked his star player for the name of the person who had contacted him. Kellogg was hesitant. "Well, gee, I can't tell you. It was a former ballplayer of yours."

"You mean Hank Poppe?" Norton had seen him hanging around the gym.

"Yes."

"What did he say again?" Norton asked.

"He said he could make me rich."

"And for just—"

"For just missing a few baskets, throwing a bad pass or two, slowing down a bit."

"A thousand dollars for that?"

"And we have to lose by more than the spread."

Norton thought for a moment. "All right," he said. "We'll take care of this. You get ready for tonight's game. Just be on the bus in a half hour."

Norton knew about a few isolated cases of "fixing" basketball games. Gamblers had been caught in the city, most notably at Brooklyn College. The coach had heard rumors this was still going on, but had no evidence. Until now.

Manhattan's game against DePaul was scheduled for the following Tuesday in Madison Square Garden in New York City. DePaul was favored by a three-point "spread," a gambling term used by people who bet on basketball games. The Blue Demons had to win by at least three points for gamblers to win their bets.

Poppe had offered Kellogg $1,000 to make sure that Manhattan lost by more than the three-point spread. The gamblers could then confidently bet on DePaul to win by more than three points, or "cover" the spread. With a star player on the hook, the gamblers had a sure thing and could win big.

Kellogg didn't know what to think as the bus carrying the Manhattan basketball team rattled along the highway toward Jersey City. His mind kept going back to that scene in his room. One thousand dollars! It was a lot of money—much more than he had ever had in his pocket. Yes, it was a lot of money. But taking it wasn't the right thing to do.

Poppe had said he would call on Sunday evening. Kellogg made up his mind not to talk to him then, or any other time. But the star player was unaware that a plot was being hatched, and he was right in the middle of it.

Norton slipped into a seat next to Kellogg on the bus.

"I'd like you to come by my office at five o'clock Sunday afternoon, Junius," Norton told Kellogg.

"It's about Poppe, isn't it?"

"Five sharp," Norton emphasized.

On Sunday afternoon, January 14, Kellogg opened the door to Norton's office. He was expecting to meet with his coach privately. Instead, he was looking at a crowded room full of strangers. He hesitated, suddenly not sure he wanted to go in.

"Now, Junie, don't be frightened," Norton said, "these people are all my friends."

Norton firmly nudged him through the door. He introduced Kellogg to his "friends"—who happened to be New York City detectives and police officers. Once again, Kellogg went through his story.

The detectives explained their plan. They instructed Kellogg to tell Poppe that he would accept the money to "throw" the game.

"When he calls you tonight," one detective said, "we'll have it switched in here. We'll monitor it. Set up a meeting with him. We'll tail you."

The plan depended on Poppe's expected call. He had told Kellogg he would be in touch by 7:30 P.M. But would he keep his word?

The waiting game began.

Norton sat at his desk, leaning his chair against the wall and shooting smoke circles in the air from his cigar. Kellogg sat nearby, nervously glancing at the telephone just inches away.

The 7:30 deadline passed. No call from Poppe.

At 8:30, still no call.

Finally, the telephone rang. Nervously, Kellogg answered. After a short pause he spoke into the receiver. "Yeah, yeah, Hank. Well, I'd like to know more about it, you know...I'd like to know more about it."

Kellogg listened a while, and hung up the phone. The conversation had lasted less than a minute.

"What did he say?" Norton asked.

"He's going to pick me up here in five minutes."

Kellogg slipped into a raincoat and started toward the door to wait for Poppe. It was raining hard, a cold January night rain. Someone shouted, "Get the cars out of there...the police cars!"

"And shut out the lights!" added a policeman.

Then Kellogg overheard one of the detectives giving orders. "Get a tail on him," he said. "Follow him. Get license plates, follow where they go." There was no turning back now. The plan was in motion.

The men practically tripped over each other as they suddenly shifted into high-speed mode. Everything had to look normal when Poppe arrived to pick up Kellogg.

Kellogg waited in the dark with Norton and one of the detectives. Everyone else was out of sight.

Headlights flashed, glaring through the rain. Poppe was at the wheel of the car. He leaned over and opened the door as Kellogg jumped in. Standing in the dark of his office, Norton heard the car accelerate and drive off. He expected to hear a police car follow shortly after. But all he heard was complete silence.

What happened next was almost like a comedy skit.

Cursing, a detective who had been hiding outside stumbled through the door into Norton's office, his clothes all muddy. In his rush to get to his car in the dark, he'd tripped over a fence and fallen head over heels, landing in the mud.

A backup detective rushed into action.

Moments later, he returned to the office. "I couldn't get the car started," the embarrassed detective said. "He was in and out and gone, and we don't know where he went."

One hour later, Kellogg returned soaking wet. He had gone to a bar with Poppe and had managed to convince him that he planned to go along with the fix. Poppe arranged to contact Kellogg prior to the game Tuesday night. He said he would give him the point spread by which Manhattan was to lose. He also warned Kellogg that it was worth his life to keep his mouth shut.

The DePaul-Manhattan clash was part of a big college basketball doubleheader at the Garden in New York. In those days, college ball was more popular than the pros. And the Garden match-ups featured some of the best teams in the country—usually a national power against a local power. DePaul and Manhattan both had strong, representative clubs. And since this was before the era of television coverage, the Garden was sure to be packed with excited fans.

Detectives expected Poppe to contact Kellogg during the afternoon while the players were resting in their hotel rooms after a practice at the Garden.

"We went down for a shoot-around in the afternoon and then went back to our hotel rooms where we would take the boys and feed them four hours before the game and then let them get off their feet and rest 'til game time," Norton remembered many years later in an interview. "Then we'd go across the street to play the ballgame."

Kellogg waited in his hotel room for Poppe's call, but it never came.

Almost game time and still no word from Poppe. Now on the floor of Madison Square Garden, as Kellogg and his teammates went through their pre-game shooting exercise, a voice rang out:

"Junius!"

The player turned to see Poppe standing at courtside, his hands in his pocket and a little smile on his face.

Kellogg nodded.

"It's thirteen points…"

Kellogg moved closer to Poppe, letting the ball bounce to the floor.

"Thirteen?"

"Yeah. Manhattan's got to lose by thirteen points,"

Junius Kellogg

Junius Kellogg is congratulated by Bronx district attorney George DeLuca in 1951, while Coach Kenny Norton looks on.

Poppe said. "On the rebounds, miss the ball occasionally, or throw hook shots over the basket. After you get the rebounds, don't pass so fast. Don't try too hard to block the other guy's shot."

The nervous Kellogg listened attentively.

"And whatever you do," Poppe added, "don't stink up the joint." He made it clear he didn't want officials to suspect that players were purposely playing badly so they could lose the game.

Kellogg's heart was thumping hard as he watched

Poppe stroll away. The star player took his position on the court. His chest tightened as he looked out at the crowd. The assistant district attorney sat in a courtside seat. Detectives and police officers were scattered throughout the building, watching every move. Poppe was sitting in the loge seats with his wife, who was wearing a fur coat.

Kellogg tried hard, maybe a little too hard. He missed his first two shots by wide margins. Coach Norton was alarmed.

Norton recalled Kellogg's inability to put the ball in the basket. "You'd think he was dumping the game, he was so nervous. Kellogg is trying so hard, and nothing can go right for the kid. I'm telling you, he's missing hangers in there."

Nothing else for Norton to do but replace him.

"Charlie, go in for Kellogg," the Manhattan coach told Charles Jennerich.

Kellogg felt a tap on his shoulder.

"Junie, I'm in for you," Jennerich said.

Kellogg walked to courtside with his head down. He mopped his face with a towel and sighed heavily.

"Take it easy, kid," Norton said to Kellogg, patting his knees.

The final score was a surprise, especially to the gamblers. Manhattan, the underdog, beat DePaul 62–59 as Jennerich, Kellogg's replacement, made all eight of his shots and finished with 17 points. Kellogg, playing only a small part in the game, scored merely four points—way below his average. It wasn't exactly what the gamblers had had in mind when they placed their "sure-thing" bets. They'd lost thousands of dollars.

Meanwhile, Kellogg still had some undercover spy work to do. Poppe had arranged a meeting with the player at Gilhooley's, a saloon, after the game. Would Kellogg still receive the $1,000 "dump" money even though his team had won? Nobody knew, but the authorities felt that Kellogg couldn't miss the opportunity of meeting with Poppe.

Before he left, Kellogg was "wired" for sound to record the conversation at his scheduled meeting. In those days, there were no inconspicuous recording devices. Police had to tape bulky wires to Kellogg's body. It was a dangerous mission. His life was worthless if the gamblers discovered the wires. Kellogg knew that, yet he summoned up enough courage to go to his appointed meeting with Poppe.

While Kellogg was waiting nervously at the tavern, however, Poppe was caught red-handed exchanging money with two gamblers. Kellogg's spy mission was canceled.

Poppe's arrest was just the beginning of a widespread gambling scandal that shook college basketball. It affected schools and players around the country. Dozens were arrested. Kellogg had blown the whistle on the biggest point-shaving scandal in college basketball history. He became a national hero.

After graduation, Kellogg signed with the Harlem Globetrotters. On April 2, 1954, he was traveling with teammates to a game in Arkansas. Suddenly, a tire blew on their car. The vehicle spun out of control and crashed. Kellogg was seriously injured—all four limbs paralyzed.

Doctors told him he would remain paralyzed from the neck down for the rest of his life. Kellogg refused to believe them.

He worked with therapists with the same kind of courage he had shown working with the authorities against the gamblers. Day by day, Kellogg improved. In four years, he was able to use his hands and arms.

Finally he was even able to play basketball again.

He helped to popularize wheelchair basketball, and he coached his team to four international championships.

After his death in 1998 at the age of 71, Kellogg was honored for his efforts on behalf of the wheelchair basketball teams and for his years of work for the New York City government. But this brave man would be remembered first, last, and always for his character and courage in helping to expose the gamblers who were threatening to undermine the sport he loved.

"When the gamblers were looking for someone to approach on the team, they picked Kellogg because he was black and underprivileged, and therefore [they thought] he would go for it," Norton, Kellogg's proud coach, once said.

"They just picked the wrong kid."

6
JIM ABBOTT
Beating the Odds

No one was talking to Jim Abbott. He sat on the bench in the New York Yankees' dugout, waiting to take the mound for the ninth inning.

It was late in the 1993 baseball season. Jim Abbott vs. the Cleveland Indians at Yankee Stadium. The Yankees were leading, 4–0. The game was going well for Jim, but he was getting the silent treatment from his teammates. Why?

It wasn't that his teammates were angry with him or didn't like him. Abbott was pitching a no-hitter. There's an unwritten rule in baseball. Never talk to anyone pitching a no-hitter. It's an old superstition. If you do, players think you can "jinx" the pitcher. You don't even want to go near a pitcher working on a no-hitter. Stay away.

Now Abbott was through eight innings. Three outs to go.

When he walked to the mound in the ninth, the crowd of 27,225 was on its feet and cheering.

Strike! Strike! Strike!

They cheered every pitch that Abbott threw. The noise got louder and louder.

New York Yankees pitcher Jim Abbott in 1993

Finally, Abbott was down to the last out. He looked toward home plate for the sign from his catcher. He wound up and fired. The batter swung and tapped a grounder to short. Out!

Silent treatment no more. Abbott was mobbed by his team-mates as they rushed to congratulate him. Only seven other Yankees had pitched no-hitters in the team's history. Now Abbott was number eight.

An impressive performance. No-hitters are rare in baseball, a cause for celebration for the winning team. In Abbott's case, it had even more of a special meaning.

Jim Abbott, you see, was born with only one hand.

Jim Abbott

Abbott didn't think he was different than any other boy in Flint, Michigan. Like many boys, he dreamed of playing professional baseball. He never gave any thought to how difficult it would be. "I just always thought it would be possible," he said.

Not everyone agreed.

"A few people told me I wouldn't go far in sports," Jim said. "I didn't listen."

Jim's father, Mike Abbott, didn't listen to the doubters either. He was determined to find ways to help his son do everything other kids did. Even small tasks that most people take for granted were challenging at first. For instance, how does one tie a shoelace with only one hand? Mike Abbott figured out a way, then taught his son how to do it. Little by little they went on to more complicated activities.

Mike didn't want his son to miss out on sports either. He took young Jim out to a park near their home and played catch with him. He taught Jim how to wear a baseball glove on his right wrist and throw with his left arm. Then, they worked out a quick switch of the glove to the left hand so Jim could take the return throw. He soon became very good at this glove-switching routine.

Jim liked playing baseball and fielding. But most of all he loved pitching. He would pretend to be Nolan Ryan, one of his favorite major league pitchers. Every day he went outside and threw the ball against the brick wall of his townhouse.

In the house, his mother heard *thump, thump, thump,*

over and over. Jim was at it again. He never missed a day of practice.

Jim made up a game for himself: Throw against the wall, move closer to the house, switch the glove to his left hand, and catch the ball. Throw again, take another step closer.

With each move, the ball came back quicker and quicker. Jim worked at it until no matter how fast the ball came back, he could make the catch. Switching the glove was a skill that would determine his future in baseball.

At school young Jim wore an artificial limb with a hook on his right arm. It made it easier for him to do some things. One day he came home from school angry and in tears. Some kids had taunted him. They called him nicknames like "Captain Hook" and "Crab." Other kids were afraid to play with him.

Jim took off the hook. He wanted to be like everyone else. He joined the baseball, football, and basketball teams. Then Jim went out for Little League baseball. He wanted to make a good impression. He did. He pitched a no-hitter in his very first Little League game!

When Jim went out for the baseball team at Flint Central High School, the coach was doubtful. Yes, he saw that Abbott had a strong left arm. But could he field his position with only one hand?

To test Jim, the coach told his hitters to lay down bunts in Abbott's direction. He wanted to see if Abbott could field his position after throwing a pitch.

Jim Abbott

Six up, six down. Abbott threw out all the batters trying to bunt for base hits. The coach was convinced. Jim had certainly perfected his glove-switching routine.

Not only that, but Abbott also played first base, shortstop, and left field when he wasn't pitching. He was a star at the plate. In his senior year, Abbott hit an above-average .427 and blasted seven home runs while batting with one hand. He also had thirty-one runs batted in (RBI).

Abbott wasn't idle during the rest of the school term. He also quarterbacked the football team and played forward on the basketball team.

But Abbott loved baseball most, especially pitching. "Pitching was my forte from the beginning," he said.

Major league scouts took notice. In Abbott's senior year in high school, a scout from the Toronto Blue Jays started showing up for the games. After watching Abbott pitch once, he kept coming back for more. He reported to his team that Abbott had a "mammoth heart." And almost as an afterthought in his report, "…no right hand."

Believe it or not, Jim got an offer to play for the Toronto Blue Jays—a major league contract!

The Abbotts had a family conference. His parents had always wanted him to go to college. Jim decided to say no to the Blue Jays and yes to the University of Michigan.

"My baseball coach, Bob Holec, told my mother that maybe I should think about a smaller college," Abbott recalled. "But I wanted a big college."

He became a Michigan Wolverine. And with a sports scholarship, no less.

"For a college coach, to let a guy with one hand play, that's really something," Abbott said of Michigan baseball coach Bud Middaugh.

In his first game at Michigan, Abbott came on in relief against North Carolina. The Tar Heels had a runner on third base.

When the Michigan catcher threw the ball back to Abbott after one pitch, the Tar Heel runner on third took off for home plate. He didn't think Jim could make the glove switch quick enough to throw him out.

Wrong. Abbott made it quicker than the North Carolina player could have imagined—much quicker. He threw out the runner by 20 feet. Abbott gained the victory when the Wolverines scored twice in the bottom of the inning.

Abbott had the glove-switching routine down to a science. Some might have been concerned that the aluminum bats used by college players would give him trouble. The ball travels faster off aluminum than it does off wood. No need to worry. Jim easily handled the rocketlike shots off the aluminum bats.

When the ball is hit right back to the mound, it is called a "comebacker." A hard-hit ball off an aluminum bat can cause serious injury if the pitcher is not ready to field it. No problem for Abbott. With one hand, he was a better fielder than many pitchers with two. Those glove-switching lessons he learned from his father were really paying off big-time!

Jim Abbott

The victory over North Carolina was the first of twenty-six for Abbott at Michigan. By the 1987 season he was the star of the Wolverines' pitching staff. He led Michigan to the Big Ten championship. He was named winner of the Golden Spikes Award as America's top amateur baseball player.

That same year, he was invited to try out for the U.S. national team that would compete at the Pan American Games. As always, Jim had his doubters. The U.S. coach was concerned about Jim's fielding. During practice he ordered his players to bunt on him to see how he handled it. Again Jim passed the test. He made the team.

Before the Pan American Games in August 1987, the U.S. team went to Cuba to play a series. Their opponents were the Cuban national team, the best amateur baseball club in the world. The Cubans won the first two games of the series before Abbott went to work in the final game. This was pressure. The Americans did not want to be embarrassed by a three-game sweep.

When Abbott took the mound, he received a standing ovation from the crowd of 50,000. Among the fans that day was Cuban president Fidel Castro.

"In Cuba, he's all they wanted to see," U.S. national team coach Ron Fraser said of Abbott. "They wanted to see how he could switch the glove and throw."

The crowd didn't have to wait long. The first Cuban batter hit a chopper 20 feet in the air down the third base line. This time, Abbott didn't have time to switch his glove. He caught the ball on the back of the glove and threw the batter out.

The big crowd gave Abbott another standing ovation.

The fans rose to their feet again after he led the Americans to victory over the powerful Cubans. It was America's first win over a Cuban national team in twenty-five years!

On to the Pan Am Games in Indianapolis, Indiana, where the American team hoped to prove that they were Olympic material. The Americans had their work cut out for them. To qualify for the 1988 Olympics in Seoul, Korea, they had to finish among the top three teams in Indianapolis by winning a gold, silver, or bronze medal.

This had been a good year for Abbott. Already the winner of the 1987 Sullivan Award, given annually to the best amateur athlete in America, he had proved wrong all the predictions that he would not go far in sports. Abbott had gone after his dreams, no matter what anyone said, and now he was getting recognition for his achievements as the first baseball player to win the Sullivan Award. When Jim was drafted by the California Angels, even his dream of playing in the major leagues had again come within his reach. But that would have to wait a little longer. First Jim wanted to win in Indianapolis and earn a chance to play in the Olympics.

At the Pan Am Games he received yet another honor. He was chosen to carry the American flag in the opening ceremonies. After leading the American athletes into the arena, Abbott led his team to a silver medal. He and his teammates were on their way to the Olympics!

Jim Abbott

California Angels rookie pitcher Jim Abbott delivers a pitch against the Boston Red Sox in 1989.

The American baseball players won their first four games and finally made it to the gold medal game. Their opponent was Japan, the defending Olympic champions, who had beaten the U.S. at the 1984 Games. No American baseball team had ever won Olympic gold.

Through a tiring exhibition schedule, Abbott had been the Americans' most reliable pitcher. Now he was given the starting role in their most important game of the year. It was strength against strength: Abbott's fastballs against Japan's outstanding fastball hitters.

Abbott was not at his best the day of the big game. He got himself into trouble in the sixth inning. The U.S. coaches thought about taking him out. But he was the Americans' best pitcher. Even though he was in a tight spot, he still had his stuff. They left him in.

Going into the bottom of the eighth inning, Abbott held a 5–3 lead. With a runner on first, Abbott wound up and fired. The Japanese hitter swung and the ball came off his bat like a rocket—a "comebacker" to Abbott.

In the blink of an eye, Abbott had switched the glove to his left hand and lunged for the hard smash. But the ball popped out of his mitt and bounced halfway toward first base.

Extending his 6-foot-3 frame to the limit, Abbott stretched out and scooped up the bouncing ball. In one quick motion he shoveled it to first baseman Tino Martinez. The toss just beat the Japanese runner by an eyelash. A great play! The Americans knew it. The Japanese knew it. Everyone in the stands knew it.

Abbott had landed hard. He was hurting, but not

enough to leave the game. He slowly picked himself up, determined to continue.

The last five Japanese hitters went down, all on ground balls. And Abbott had pitched—and fielded—the U.S. to the gold medal! After retiring the last batter, Abbott leaped in the air. As he hit the ground his happy teammates piled on top of him in celebration.

It was a golden moment for Jim. "It was my dream of a lifetime," he said.

One of the best things about a team sport is being able to share such winning feelings. There were more winning feelings ahead for Jim Abbott.

Unlike most players, Abbott bypassed the minor leagues and went straight to the majors, signing with the California Angels. In his first year he pitched two shutouts—one of them against Cy Young winner Roger Clemens. With twelve victories in 1989, he set a record for major league rookies who had never played in the minors.

In his major league career, Abbott played for the California Angels, New York Yankees, Chicago White Sox, and Milwaukee Brewers. When he retired in 1999, he had won eighty-seven games. The highlight: the no-hitter for the Yankees in 1993.

After that game, the Yankee Stadium grounds crew dug up the pitching rubber. They asked all of Abbott's Yankee teammates to sign it and gave it to him as a souvenir. The Hall of Fame also wanted a souvenir of the performance—

Abbott's hat and a baseball from the game.

Jim Abbott had left more than a legacy of great performances, though. He had given hope to anyone facing impossible odds.

"My hand hasn't kept me from doing anything I wanted to do," he said. "I believe you can do anything you want, if you put your mind to it."

7
JANET GUTHRIE
Lady in the Fast Lane

*R*ace time. Janet Guthrie strapped herself into the seat of her car. She nervously looked down the long oval track ahead of her.

The year: 1977.

The place: the Indianapolis Motor Speedway.

The mission: to become the first woman to qualify to compete in the Indy 500.

She'd turned in the fastest lap of any driver on the first day of practice. Now she was ready for another practice run. A good showing today would clinch one of thirty-three spots in the big Memorial Day race.

"Iron will"—that's the way her father described his daughter as a young girl. And now, after a long, hard struggle, she had finally arrived! She had made a courageous stand against the men that ruled the sport. Now people recognized her as a full-fledged race driver. But she hadn't yet achieved her ultimate goal.

Guthrie had failed in her attempt to qualify for the 1976 Indy 500. The car just wasn't fast enough. But this year she had a new, speedier car—the "Lightning Offenhauser."

Janet Guthrie, the first woman to qualify to compete in
the Indianapolis 500

It was late afternoon on May 10, and Guthrie was ready to test herself again. She got off to a good start.

But as she took her second turn around the track, there was trouble. When she tried to make a left turn on the banked wall, she lost control of her car. Officials clocked her at 191 miles per hour just before she crashed into the wall.

Janet Guthrie

Everyone at the track held his breath. Emergency crews rushed to the crash site.

To everyone's astonishment, Guthrie came out of the car unhurt.

The car was so badly damaged that it would have to be rebuilt. Could it be restored to its former levels of speed and performance so that Guthrie would be able to qualify for this year's race? And what about Guthrie? She had already shown her courage by breaking into the all-male racing world. After this devastating setback, would she be brave enough to race again?

It was no surprise that Janet Guthrie excelled at one of the most dangerous sports on earth. She had always loved adventure and daring new experiences.

Janet was born on March 7, 1938, in Iowa City, Iowa, and lived on a farm for the first few years of her life. Her father, an airline pilot, later moved the family to South Florida, where Janet took up flying.

At thirteen, she had already flown an airplane. At age sixteen, Janet decided she wanted to try a free-fall parachute jump. In free-fall, the parachutist jumps out of a plane without opening the chute. After falling several hundred feet at more than 100 miles an hour, the cord is pulled to open the chute. Then, if all goes well, the parachutist floats safely to the ground.

Her father wouldn't hear of it. "Absolutely not," he said. "No free-fall!"

But Janet persisted. Finally, her father gave in. "Just one

time," he said, "but you have to be careful and do it the right way."

He would allow her to jump only on two conditions: He would fly the plane and she would receive parachuting lessons before the jump.

Since there were no parachuting schools in South Florida at the time, Janet's father hired a pro to give her private lessons. In her autobiography, *Janet Guthrie—A Life at Full Throttle*, Janet said the pro taught her how to pull the rip cord that opened the chute, how to absorb the shock after landing, and how to fasten the helmet so it wouldn't fly off.

Janet then did some practicing of her own: She propped a ladder against the side of her house. First she jumped off a low rung of the ladder. Then she climbed higher and jumped again. Finally, she took a flying leap from the roof. She was lucky. Safe landing every time.

Her father then flew the plane for his adventurous daughter. She jumped. Safe landing again—just like jumping off the roof of her house.

Would her father let her do it again?

"Never again," he vowed.

"It was too hard on him," Guthrie said.

By the time she was twenty-one, she had earned a commercial pilot's license. She flew whenever she could break away from her classes at the University of Michigan.

After graduating, Guthrie got a job as a physicist in the aerospace industry. She saved her money for an entire year and bought a car. Guthrie wasn't satisfied with just any car.

She chose a Jaguar XK 120—the sleek and popular sports car that she had dreamed about since she was a teenager.

At first Guthrie enjoyed just driving the car around Long Island, outside New York City. Then she heard about a local sports car club where members could compete. She loved her car and wanted to see how it would do on a track. Soon she was entering races—and winning them.

Excited by her success, Guthrie attended a driving school in Connecticut. She was a natural. Her instructor, veteran driver Gordon McKenzie, liked the way she handled her car. He suggested she try auto racing.

A thrill shot through Guthrie. What a great idea. Off she went to enroll in a racing car drivers' school sponsored by the Sports Car Club of America (SCCA). Guthrie swapped her Jaguar for a higher-priced model built especially for racing—the XK 140. Before long she had taught herself how to take apart and rebuild its engine like a pro.

Most of the people who raced were rich. Guthrie wasn't. After spending her money on car parts, she often didn't have enough left for a hotel room. But she wasn't going to give up racing.

Once again she came up with a plan. When she was traveling the racing circuit, she would save money by sleeping in the back of her station wagon.

"I could always use the track restroom to get all spiffed up and go out to dinner," she said. "Then I'd come back and get in my sleeping bag in the station wagon."

In time the wagon became more than a home. It was her

workshop—a sort of moveable garage. She even built her engines there.

Racing was taking up more and more of her life. Finally she quit her job as a physicist. She bought another car, a Toyota Celica. Working twelve to fourteen hours a day, seven days a week, she rebuilt the car.

Guthrie's career started to pick up speed.

She entered races all over the United States, finishing in some of the country's most celebrated long-distance competitions. In 1973, she won the North Atlantic Road Racing Championship. A champion, yes, but a tired champion. By then she had been racing for thirteen years. She was exhausted, broke, and thinking of leaving the sport.

That's when she got the phone call. Someone named Vollstedt was asking her to drive his car in the 1976 Indy 500. No woman had ever driven in that race. *This has to be a prank,* thought Guthrie. But Vollstedt, an auto designer and builder from Oregon, wasn't kidding. Could she drive a "championship" car? That was the big question.

With their open cockpits, wide wheelbases, and rear engines, championship cars were much different than the closed sports cars Guthrie had been accustomed to driving for many years.

"Before she would agree to drive for me," Vollstedt said, "she wanted to see if she could handle the car."

Vollstedt was wondering the same thing, too. He arranged for a secret test at the Ontario Motor Speedway near Los Angeles.

Janet Guthrie

To get into top physical shape for Vollstedt's test, Guthrie did exercises in front of her TV. One day she lost her balance, landed hard on her left foot, and fell to the floor. The doctors told her she had broken a bone and they put her foot in a heavy cast. *How am I going to drive a racing car?* she worried. *Will I miss my big chance?*

As test time approached, Guthrie became more and more nervous. She knew she couldn't drive with the cast on her foot, but every doctor she consulted told her it was too soon to take it off. Desperate, she decided to do it herself. She soaked the cast in water and peeled it off. Then she put a bandage around the foot.

"All I could think was, 'I've got my hands on an Indianapolis car.' There was no way I was going to show up on crutches," Guthrie said. When Vollstedt asked her why she was limping, Guthrie told him she had sprained her ankle.

Broken ankle and all, Guthrie stepped into an unfamiliar car. She hit the accelerator. When her car got up to speed, Guthrie couldn't believe the feeling. "What a thrill," she said. "It was like going to the moon."

Vollstedt was impressed with her time—an average speed of 178.52 miles per hour and a top speed of 196 mph.

Test passed.

She had showed Vollstedt she could drive the car. Now she had to show the rest of the world.

Next Guthrie was going for another test—the trials for the Indianapolis 500. She only had a few weeks to get ready.

Guthrie was concerned about the fatigue factor of driving in a 500-mile race.

"I've been doing isometric exercises to strengthen my neck muscles and a bit of jogging," she said about her preparation for Indy. "I've driven heavy cars such as sedans on tight courses where there is little time to relax. I'll be in shape."

To further prepare for her big chance, Janet Guthrie entered the Trenton 200, the last big race before the 1976 Indy. The track at Trenton was very similar to Indy—long and oval.

She felt ready. She sat in her blue racing car, wearing her white helmet with the black letters spelling JAN.

"Janet and Gentlemen, start your engines," said the announcer.

The cars roared down the speedway.

Suddenly one of Guthrie's pit crew shouted, "She's coming in!"

The chinstrap on her helmet had loosened. "Of all the dumb things that had to happen," she said to the crewman who rushed over to her. He tightened it and she was off again.

On another lap, she spun out avoiding a faster car and damaged her gearbox. She lost fourth gear. Frustrated and disappointed, she was forced out of the race.

How she would do at the Indy 500, the biggest race of all, was anybody's guess.

Some of the drivers didn't think a woman belonged in

Janet Guthrie waits in her racecar as her pit crew works.

the Indy 500. Bobby Unser, an Indianapolis 500 winner, said, "I could take a hitchhiker and teach him how to drive better than Janet Guthrie."

As the first woman picked for the Indy 500, Guthrie faced fierce opposition. Many people were convinced that there were good reasons to exclude women from racing. *It's too dangerous for women to drive a racing car,* they said. *A female driver could cause accidents. Women do not have the physical and mental stamina that men have. A woman can't control a car going at 200 miles an hour.*

It was up to Guthrie to prove them wrong.

The following month, Guthrie took to the track to try to

qualify at Indy. She was a rookie driver with a lot to learn. She wasn't used to the huge oval track and its high concrete walls.

Like most rookies, she shied away from the steep, banked walls. They were scary; one slip could be fatal. Before she could race in the Indy 500, though, Guthrie had to be able to handle them.

When she came back from her first practice run, she was furious with herself. The walls still terrified her. Dick Simon, her teammate, took out a pencil and paper. He showed her how to come out of the turns going right up to the outside wall.

She was determined to do it right. No wall would stop her. She borrowed a car and stuck a four-inch welding rod in the door. Over and over again, she went around the track, faster and faster, closer and closer, until she heard the metal scrape against the wall. She kept driving until she wore down the rod. She was going so fast, driving so close to the wall, the professionals watching were scared for her.

Good, but not good enough. Guthrie failed to qualify.

The following year, 1977, she was at it again at Indy, more resolute than ever. But then came the devastating crash of her Lightning Offenhauser. Her dream car was a wreck, but she refused to give up.

Guthrie's crew worked on the damaged car for several days. They knew the car would never be the same, but they kept working on it. Finally, they told her they'd done all they could.

Janet Guthrie

Before the crack-up, the Lightning Offenhauser was in top form. But how would it perform now?

Guthrie waited on the track before the qualifying round for the 1977 Indy 500. She gunned the motor. The flag went down and her car took off. As she picked up speed, witnesses were amazed at how skillfully and coolly she handled the wheel. She sped four laps around the Indy track, going faster each lap. No crack-ups this time. When she pulled to a halt after the fourth sizzling lap, Guthrie had put together an impressive average speed of 188.403 mph.

A woman had finally qualified for the Indy 500!

One week later, Guthrie climbed into her white and green "Lightning Offy" and drove onto the starting line of the world-famous Indianapolis 500. Merely by sitting in her car on the track she had made a meaningful breakthrough.

Before that historic moment, the Indy track had been strictly off-limits to women. Females hadn't been allowed in the pits where the cars were repaired and refueled during the grueling race. They hadn't even been permitted in the press box!

Guthrie strapped on her white helmet and crossed her fingers. Her car's brand-new engine hadn't been fully tested. Hopefully, though, there would be no problems.

At the sound of the announcer's voice, the thirty-three drivers started their engines. Off they went in a blaze of smoke and noise. The crowd roared with excitement.

Guthrie knew something was wrong on the first lap.

"I held up my hand to the crew," she said. "It was

thumbs down. And when I got to the back straight [the engine] started missing and I told them [by radio communication] that I was coming in because something serious was wrong."

As she pulled into the pit stop, the engine was sputtering. The crew worked furiously on the engine and soon sent her back out on the track.

It wasn't long before Guthrie was in the pit again. A fuel mixture of alcohol and methanol had spilled out of the engine, soaking her as she sat in the bucket seat. Quickly, her pit crew doused her with water to dilute the fuel. It was a little help. The fuel mixture had soaked through her blue and white driving suit onto her skin. It was blazing hot in the pits. Guthrie's skin was burning. But she remained calm and returned to the race.

Soon, another problem and another pit stop. This time, the car needed a new ignition system.

Other drivers with car problems had already dropped out of the race. Not Guthrie. "If they fix the car," she declared, "I'll get back in the race and run like I was never out of it."

This time, Guthrie had to get out of the car while the pit crew attempted to fix the problem. Her skin still burned from the fuel. She sat on a stack of tires and poured more water over herself.

Out on the track once more.

"You can't call her a quitter," a woman near the pit said. "I'd have been crying by now."

Janet Guthrie

Guthrie made five more pit stops before finally giving up. "Each time they replaced an element in the car," she said later, "the thought was, 'I'll try it out.' But after two or three times, we knew it was no use."

Guthrie may not have finished, but she proved she belonged. With her never-say-die attitude, she was sure to be back.

In 1978, Janet Guthrie returned to Indy. This time, she finished the race. And she did it with one hand! Driving with a broken right wrist and on painkillers, Guthrie wound up ninth among the thirty-three drivers.

At the beginning Janet Guthrie had faced open hostility from many of the drivers. Now, thanks to her courageous performance, she was welcomed as one of them.

"The whole thing is an adventure," she said. "You extend yourself to the last limit of strength and endurance and spirit—and then you go farther."

8
JACKIE ROBINSON
The First

*B*ranch Rickey, the general manager of the Brooklyn Dodgers *and a man with a sharp eye for sports potential, had a secret. It was 1947, and Rickey knew that what he was planning would cause an uproar.*

At that time every single player in the major leagues was white. Blacks played in a separate league called the Negro Leagues. Rickey was looking for baseball talent and he couldn't see why he should limit his search. He had decided to bring a black player into white baseball. Pretending that he was going to start a black baseball team in Brooklyn, he invited Jackie Robinson to a meeting.

Robinson, a star in the Negro Leagues, came to the secret meeting with Rickey expecting to be asked to join the new "Brooklyn Brown Dodgers." Imagine his surprise when he heard Rickey say, "I think you can play in the major leagues."

Robinson was stunned. Was it a dream? No. It wasn't a dream, but there was a catch. Rickey told Robinson that he would have to follow certain guidelines if he joined the team. One of them: no fighting, even if pushed to the limit. Ricky gave Robinson an example. "Suppose I collide with you at second base?" he asked.

Jackie Robinson of the Brooklyn Dodgers at Ebbets Field in 1947

"When I get up, I yell, 'You dirty, black—!' What do you do?"

Robinson was confused. "Mr. Rickey," he asked, "do you want a ballplayer who's afraid to fight back?"

"I want a player with guts enough NOT to fight back," Rickey explained. "You've got to do this job with base hits and stolen bases and by fielding ground balls, Jackie. Nothing else."

For years, bigoted whites had been saying that blacks shouldn't *play in the big leagues. They didn't have the talent, people said. Black players couldn't stand the pressure. They would fail.*

Rickey was afraid if there was an incident of any kind, it would prove these opponents right. An angry outburst from Robinson could ruin Rickey's plans to integrate baseball.

"One incident, just one incident, can set it back twenty years," Rickey said.

Robinson knew what a momentous opportunity this was. Baseball wasn't the only segregated professional sport in America. The National Basketball Association was all white too. And the National Football League, which had been integrated many years earlier with a handful of blacks, was slow in bringing African American players into the league during that time.

Rickey was asking Robinson to take on a controversial and risky challenge. A lot of people would be enraged to see Robinson on the field. They would criticize and mock him and he would not be able to defend himself. Robinson would have to let his performance on the field convince the doubters.

Should he take on the challenge?

Jackie Robinson was born in Cairo, Georgia, in 1919, the grandson of a slave. Although slavery had been outlawed after the Civil War, conditions for blacks in the South hadn't improved much in two generations.

Robinson's mother, Maille, moved her five children to Pasadena, California, in hopes of a better life for all of them. Not long after their arrival, the Robinsons found that they had escaped from the South but not from prejudice.

"When we moved into a white neighborhood," Robinson

once remembered, "our neighbors tried to force us to move away." Some neighbors threw rocks at Robinson; others cursed at him.

But Maille Robinson decided to keep her family in Pasadena. There were good reasons to stay. First, she knew that her children had a better chance to get a good education in California. Second, she had relatives in the city who could help her raise her children. She supported the family by working tirelessly at manual labor. As the kids got older, they chipped in, too.

"It was still a constant struggle to make ends meet," Robinson said, "but we kids began to help out by doing odd jobs and, at the same time, we were going to schools—good schools. That was what Mother had set her heart on."

Robinson, who was only eighteen months old when he was taken to California, developed a strong circle of friends as he grew up in Pasadena. One hot summer day Robinson and his friends took off for the town's public pool. But when they showed up in their bathing suits, they were turned away. "Sorry," said someone at the gate, "this is a whites-only swimming day." In fact, six days of the week were reserved strictly for whites. Blacks were allowed to swim there only on the one remaining day.

So Robinson and his buddies headed for the town reservoir. Wrong choice again. A sheriff showed up and told them it was illegal to swim in the reservoir. Then, all of the boys were arrested and taken to jail. The terrible injustice of that day would remain with Robinson for a long time.

Being black meant you often had to face extra difficulties, but when it came to sports, Robinson's skin color didn't seem to matter. He was usually the first picked for any neighborhood team. He was simply the best athlete around.

Jackie Robinson was not just good at playing games. He could run faster than just about anyone he knew. Anyone, that is, but his brother. Mack Robinson, a track star who had broken world records and competed in the 1936 Olympics, was now internationally known. He set a high standard for his younger brother to follow. But Jackie was up to the challenge. At UCLA (the University of California at Los Angeles), he starred in football, basketball, track, and baseball. In 1941, he played a year of professional football before he was drafted into the Army.

Robinson wasn't content to just be a rank-and-file soldier. He planned to be an officer. But when he applied to the Officer's Candidate School at Fort Riley, Kansas, where he was stationed, he was turned down. The reason? He was black.

Enter Joe Louis, world heavyweight boxing champion, who also happened to be stationed at Fort Riley. He had heard about Robinson's plight. One word from the champ, and all of a sudden Robinson was in! Faster than you could say Jackie Robinson, he was sporting second lieutenant's bars.

But despite those gold bars, Robinson was not always

treated with respect. Boarding a military bus at Fort Hood, Texas, Robinson was told by the driver to sit in the back. Blacks had to sit in the rear seats, often in overcrowded conditions, even when there was plenty of room up front.

The young black officer refused, and he was brought before a military court for punishment. The Army's case, however, quickly fell apart. A recent Army order had outlawed segregation in the military. Robinson received an honorable discharge.

Robinson soon joined the Kansas City Monarchs and established himself as one of the best players in the Negro Leagues. As a shortstop, he was a sensational all-around performer who could hit, field, and steal bases. In the 1945 season, he batted a solid .340 and fielded "sensationally," according to one national magazine. In an exhibition game against an all-white team, Robinson amazed the crowd by cracking two doubles off Cleveland's great pitcher, Bob Feller. Robinson was no youngster, already twenty-seven years old, when Branch Rickey came calling.

The star shortstop considered Rickey's offer. He would be carrying a lot on his shoulders. Being the only black player in major league baseball would take courage and determination. But it would mean opening the doors for other black athletes.

Robinson was aware that the Dodgers had thoroughly researched his background. They had read of his success in four sports in college and of his service as an officer in the U.S. Army. They had followed his impressive career as a shortstop for the Kansas City Monarchs. Rickey knew that Robinson was a top athlete—but an athlete whose temper flared quickly when he was faced with racism.

Many times while traveling through the South with the Monarchs, Robinson had allowed his temper to get the better of him. In the South he constantly encountered discrimination against blacks. Separate hotels for blacks, separate restrooms, and even separate water fountains. He hated the unfairness of it all. Could he hold his feelings in on the baseball field?

History was waiting.

"Mr. Rickey," said Robinson finally, "I think I can play ball in Brooklyn. If you want to take this gamble, I promise you there will be no incident."

Rickey signed Robinson up, but first the player had to prove himself with the Royals, the Dodgers' top minor league team in Montreal. Then, if all went well, Rickey would bring him up to the major leagues with the Dodgers.

When Robinson arrived in the Canadian city, he was hardly welcomed with open arms. Royals manager Clay Hopper was not happy to have him on the team. Fans screamed racial taunts. Opposing players called him dirty names. And to make matters worse, after his first few games, Robinson went into a slump.

The constant pressure made Robinson sick. He developed a stomach problem. His hair began turning prematurely gray. Doctors told him to stay away from the ballpark for a week to rest. Robinson stayed home, but only for one day. He wanted to play baseball, not sit in his house. His wife Rachel was convinced that his problems "came from his not being able to fight back."

But he battled back with his bat. Slump over, Robinson led the International League in batting. He led all second basemen in fielding. He led the Royals to the pennant and then to victory in the Junior World Series against Louisville. He converted Hopper, his teammates, and the fans.

In the victory celebration, the delirious Royals fans carried Robinson on their shoulders to the team's locker room. Hopper shook Robinson's hand. "You're a real ballplayer and a gentleman. It's been wonderful having you on the team."

Next stop: Brooklyn.

The stage was set for his Dodger debut. A twenty-eight-year-old rookie, Jackie Robinson had won a spot on the Dodgers roster. The news hit America like a bombshell. The black community all over the country could see doors opening. Opponents were outraged and determined to do something about it.

In the Dodgers locker room, trouble was brewing. Outfielder Dixie Walker asked his teammates to sign a formal complaint. If Jackie Robinson comes, the petition stated, we want to be traded. Some of the Dodgers signed. But not Pee Wee Reese.

"If he can take my job," Dodger shortstop Reese had said of Robinson, "he's entitled to it."

When Dodgers manager Leo Durocher found out about

the petition, he was furious. Durocher said he didn't care if Robinson was green, black, or yellow—or had stripes like a zebra—he was going to be a Dodger. "I'm the manager of this team and I say he plays." The petition died.

Reese kept his job at shortstop. Durocher handed Robinson a first baseman's mitt and told him to go play the bag. "And he had never played first base," said teammate Rex Barney. "He took it and never said a word, never complained."

Robinson was a little unsteady at the position at first. But he learned quickly.

He made his first appearance as a Dodger on April 15, 1947. A crowd of more than 26,000, many of them African Americans, watched the Dodgers open the season at Ebbets Field with a 5–3 victory over the Boston Braves. Robinson went hitless, but the crowd cheered his every move. "Jackie! Jackie! Jackie!" the fans shouted.

Robinson got a different reception when the Dodgers visited Philadelphia on their first road trip of the season. The management at the hotel where they usually stayed said there were no rooms available. The Dodgers were told not to come back. The reason: Robinson, a black man, was not welcome there. The team quickly solved that problem by switching hotels.

The Dodgers couldn't easily solve another problem: Ben Chapman, the Phillies' manager. At the game that night, Chapman constantly screamed curses and personal insults at Robinson. He warned the Dodger players that they would contract diseases if they touched Robinson. He told Robinson to go back to the South and pick cotton and clean out toilets because that's all he was good for. Following the lead of their manager, the Philadelphia players echoed the insults.

Robinson took the terrible torrent of abuse silently. Not the rest of the Dodgers. Even Eddie Stanky, who had signed the petition against Robinson, was now sticking up for him. "Why don't you yell at somebody who can answer back!" Stanky screamed at the Phillies dugout.

Robinson was almost ready to walk over to the Phillies dugout and smash someone's teeth in with his "despised" black fist. But he had promised Rickey two years of not fighting back. He held in his emotions and stayed cool.

The Dodgers protested the Phillies' behavior to National League president Ford Frick. He ordered Chapman and the Phillies to stop their verbal attacks immediately. That situation was brought under control, but the Dodgers had a long season ahead of them.

Life was not easy for the Dodgers' new first baseman. He received hate mail. His life was threatened. Pitchers threw at his head. Players spit on him. They purposely aimed at Robinson with their spiked shoes as they crossed the first base bag.

It didn't seem to matter to Robinson. The more he was pushed, it seemed, the harder he played. He was playing not for himself—but for an entire race.

Jackie Robinson

Jackie Robinson plays first base for the Dodgers at Ebbets Field in 1947.

And fans, both black and white, loved him. Black fans chartered buses called the "Jackie Robinson Specials" that traveled hundreds of miles just to see him play. Brooklynites flocked to the games to cheer their new hero.

And he was fun to watch. He brought an exciting new style to the game. It would soon be known as "Dodger Baseball."

Pity the poor pitcher who allowed Robinson to get to first base. Oh, but the hometown fans loved it. Robinson would dance off the bag, fistfuls of dirt in each hand, taunting the pitcher. Every time the pitcher looked over, Robinson would be a little farther off the bag, inching closer,

closer to second. The entire stadium roared as the fans watched the pitcher finally throw over to first. Too late— Robinson had already stolen second.

Stealing home was his specialty. No one did it with more flair than Robinson.

Need a bunt? Robinson would lay down one perfectly. A great defensive play? You could count on Jackie. A game-winning hit? Leave it up to the dazzling Dodger rookie. He was the ultimate team player, usually providing just what was needed to win.

But the abuse continued. Later in the season, the Dodgers were in Cincinnati for a series with the Reds. The Dodgers were in the field. Both the Reds players and their fans were booing and cursing at Robinson. He tried to ignore the screams and concentrate on the game.

Pee Wee Reese had seen this behavior many times. Finally, he was fed up. He called time out. With the entire stadium watching, Reese walked over to Robinson. He placed his hand on his shoulder and stared back at the hecklers. The heckling slowed and then stopped under his relentless gaze. Then Reese trotted back to his position at shortstop.

"Something in my gut reacted to the moment," Reese said. "Something about—what?—the unfairness of it? The injustice of it? I don't know."

Reese was a local hero, having grown up just across the border in neighboring Kentucky. That public display of friendship not only made Robinson feel better, but it was also a symbolic gesture to everyone in the stands. In that one quiet act, Reese had answered all the racist noise in the ballpark that day.

And the Dodgers were ahead in the standings, well on their way to the National League pennant.

Baseball was in an uproar. It seemed there was a new crisis every day involving Robinson. A rumor began circulating that the St. Louis Cardinals were threatening to strike if Robinson played against them. Again, National League president Frick acted quickly. He vowed that anyone involved in such a plan would be suspended from baseball. The threat soon blew over.

The Dodgers won the pennant. And Robinson, playing an unfamiliar position at first base, was named the National League's Rookie of the Year by the *Sporting News*. It was the same newspaper that had opposed integration of baseball. The same newspaper that had once claimed, "There is not a single Negro player with major league possibilities."

Rickey, meanwhile, was busy gathering more talent from the Negro Leagues. By the end of the 1947 season, he had signed sixteen more black players for the Dodgers.

Other big league teams, seeing the wisdom of his actions, joined in the hunt for black talent. In a little over a decade, every team in the big leagues was integrated.

Robinson's success inspired trailblazers in other American sports. Soon the first trickle of black players began to appear in the National Basketball Association. That trickle eventually became a flood. More black players began appearing in the National Football League.

Sports wasn't the only part of American society affected by Robinson's breakthrough in 1947. Seven years after Jackie Robinson integrated major league baseball, the Supreme Court declared school segregation illegal. The civil rights movement expanded. Dr. Martin Luther King Jr. called Jackie Robinson "an inspiration."

After a couple of years, Robinson was a Dodger icon. No longer under orders to keep quiet, he played with a fury unmatched in all of baseball. He became one of the most combative and competitive players in the game, unafraid to hurl back insults at his enemies or speak up about social issues.

Robinson played ten years in Brooklyn, helping the Dodgers win six pennants and their first World Series championship. He had done it all: He'd won the Most Valuable Player award, led the league in batting, and finished with an above-average lifetime mark of .311.

An All-Star. A Hall of Famer.

An extraordinary career, but not his greatest legacy. As Robinson always believed, the importance of a man's life is measured not in his fame or his successes, but in the impact it has on other people's lives.

Jackie Robinson certainly had that impact.

9
GAIL DEVERS
Golden Girl

Gail Devers leans into the starting blocks, ready to spring into action. The women's 100-meter race at the 1992 Olympics in Barcelona, Spain, is about to begin. Gail is ready for the biggest race of her life.

Now is the time for Gail to show the world that she is back as one of track's brilliant young stars. Just as importantly, Gail has to show herself that she is ready for her comeback. All of her hopes and dreams are wrapped up in this race.

With Gail and the other four runners ready to push off, the crowd falls into a hush.

Then, the crack of the starter's pistol splits the silence.

They're off!

The swiftest female runners in the world take off down the track. Gail gets off to a strong start, stride for stride with the leaders. Her face is a mask of determination.

Is it all a miracle? Anyone who knows Gail's story couldn't help but ask that question.

Gail Devers displays her gold medal from the 2003 World Indoor Athletics Championships.

The "miracle girl" grew up in a household that emphasized reading, religion, and good behavior. Gail's father was a minister at a church in San Diego, California. Her mother worked in the neighborhood elementary school. Gail wanted to be a teacher just like her mom.

"We had picnics, rode bikes, and played touch football together," Gail said. "We did Bible Studies together. My father and brother played the guitar together."

Gail had an older brother named Parenthesis—nick-named PD—who loved to race. He often challenged Gail to race against him. And, oh, how he gloated when he won. He teased her so much that Gail was determined to beat him. She started to practice.

Gail Devers

The next time they raced, PD was in for a surprise. His little sister beat him. He never raced her again.

"From then on, running was all that mattered," Devers said.

As Gail grew older, she got faster and faster. At Sweetwater High School in San Diego, Gail joined the track team and quickly took on a leading role.

In 1984, her senior year, the impressive runner represented her school at the state track meet. She won the state championship in two races—the 100-meter sprint and the 100-meter hurdles.

After the meet, a broad-shouldered, athletic-looking man approached Gail and introduced himself. It was Bob Kersee, famed track coach at the University of California at Los Angeles (UCLA). This man had coached some of the world's greatest female runners. And now he was saying that he wanted Gail to come to UCLA where he could coach her too.

Kersee had big plans for Gail. He told her she could be in the Olympics and that she could win a gold medal. He said that she could break the American record in the 100-meter hurdles.

Gail was skeptical at first. "He had all these visions of years and years ahead," she said. "I could see he was crazy."

But Gail knew he could make her a better runner. Look at what he had done for his wife, track great Jackie Joyner-Kersee.

"I hadn't had much coaching," she said. "So I thought

that if he had all this faith in me, he'd coach me well. For quite a while Bobby believed in me more than I believed in myself."

Next stop for Gail: UCLA.

Day by day under Kersee's watchful gaze, Gail's times got better in the 100-meter hurdles and 100-meter race.

"My friends tease me because I only know one speed—fast," Devers said. "I run fast, talk fast, and even sleep fast!"

Fast, faster, fastest.

"It may take a while for the bulb to go on in Gail's head," Kersee said, "but once it does, and she sees what she can do, she's unstoppable."

And so she was. Gail won the National Collegiate Athletic Association's (NCAA) 100-meter dash as a senior in 1988. She set an NCAA record in the 100-meter hurdles. Bob Kersee was correct in his prediction!

And at the end of her senior year, Gail was selected for the U.S. women's Olympic track team. Her ultimate dream was coming true. But she had more work to do before she headed to Seoul, Korea, for the 1988 Summer Games.

The training schedule was incredibly demanding.

A typical day for Gail:

Out of the door by 7 A.M.

Run 100-meter sprints—nearly the length of a football field—for three hours.

Take a short break for a light lunch.

Two more hours of running.

A three-hour workout lifting iron in the weight room.

Gail Devers

Gail Devers clears a hurdle during the Golden League athletics meeting in 2002.

Gail didn't mind the grueling pace. She knew it was all part of the Olympic preparation. But while training, she started to have health problems: migraine headaches, fainting spells, and frequent vision loss. She felt constantly exhausted. She thought it was because she was overworking herself.

In Korea, Gail made it to the semifinals of the 100-yard hurdles, her specialty. But she still wasn't feeling exactly like herself. She felt weak.

Gail failed to qualify for the finals. Her dream had become a nightmare.

Good-bye, Olympics.

Good-bye, gold medal dreams.

Gail sensed that her poor performance was not just bad luck. She wasn't feeling well. Something was wrong—terribly wrong. And her condition was worsening. Soon her feet became blistered and swollen. The skin on her feet started to crack and bleed. The usually powerful runner tired too easily. Her long fingernails had recently become brittle. They started breaking and not growing back.

Could this be the first sign of a serious problem?

Gail returned to America and continued to train under Kersee's watchful eye. But she wasn't the same runner who had dominated at UCLA.

One day, Gail stumbled on the track. She couldn't run. She felt sick.

Her doctor couldn't figure out what was wrong. He advised her to get more rest. Gail was baffled. She'd always been healthy. She'd never missed a day of school, from kindergarten to twelfth grade. Why was she feeling so weak now? Why was she losing so much weight? Why was her hair falling out in clumps? Fighting off depression and disregarding her doctor's advice, she continued to train with Kersee.

Gail Devers

Her coach was worried about her. "What's wrong?" he asked.

"I don't know," she told him. "I've lost my strength. I've lost weight. I've had terrible migraine headaches."

Gail held out her hands.

They were shaking.

Kersee decided not to let her run anymore. He tried to help her gain back her energy.

"He was cooking up piles of ribs and steak and putting it on my plate, and feeding me protein shakes and everything," Gail said, "and still I didn't gain any weight."

Gail went to see another doctor. Then another. For more than two and a half years they all told her she was fine. "You're an athlete," they said. "Just take some time off."

But Gail was not feeling fine. Her mysterious ailment had gotten worse. Her skin was peeling and scaly, spotted with white.

"I went from glamour to monster," Devers said. "I covered my mirrors. I got black mini-blinds on all my windows. I was depressed."

Finally, a doctor discovered the answer. Gail had a thyroid disorder called Graves' disease. The thyroid, a butterfly-shaped gland in the neck, helps control energy level as well as weight.

Gail had a name for her illness. Now she looked forward to getting the treatment to cure it. She would undergo radiation treatments.

But instead of helping, the radiation treatments made things worse. The strong doses of radiation affected her thyroid gland. Then her feet began to hurt. Painful sores appeared on them. She had developed a terrible infection.

Still, she insisted on going back to the track. She couldn't stop running any more than she could stop breathing. Running was Gail's life.

To cushion her tender, swollen feet, Gail put on five pairs of socks. She had to wear size 12 men's running shoes.

Fellow runners didn't know about her condition. They simply wondered if her feet had grown bigger.

All her efforts were of no use. Running was still sheer agony. Gail finally had to give it up.

In the hospital, doctors examined her inflamed feet. They warned her that the spreading infection was serious. Gail was frightened. Would amputation be necessary to save her life? *No way,* she thought. *I need these feet to run.*

She found a new doctor. He prescribed a different kind of medication—an antibiotic to kill the bacteria that were causing the disease.

In a few days, Gail was feeling better. The swelling in her feet was starting to go down. She had to use a wheelchair to get around, but her feet were saved!

In one month, she was able to walk.

That was amazing enough—but soon she was running in a track meet!

By 1991, Gail had fully recovered. She entered the world championships in Tokyo and finished second in the 100-meter hurdles.

Gail Devers

The 1992 Olympics were coming up soon. Could Gail make it this time? Could she win a gold medal at the 1992 Games in Barcelona and make her dreams come true?

It was a miraculous story. And everyone in the crowd was waiting to see how it would turn out.

"My track career was sidelined," Gail said, "but my Olympic dreams never died."

She had gone from a wheelchair to crutches and then to the track. Now she had a chance to prove she was the fastest woman in the 100-meter race.

Gail was nervous. And she was scared. In the qualifying rounds, she felt awkward. As she positioned herself for one of the heats, she lost feeling in her legs. Had her Graves' disease suddenly returned?

"I had complete numbness from my hip down," Gail said. "I couldn't feel my right leg." She was understandably upset.

Kersee came over to give her a pep talk, then gave her instructions. "This is the Olympic Games," the coach said. "You can't feel your leg, so drive ahead with your arms. You can feel them."

His advice worked! Gail qualified for the finals.

It turned out to be the closest women's 100-meter race in Olympic history. Everyone in the Olympic Stadium waited breathless minutes for the results to be announced. No one knew who had won.

Finally, the results were announced.

The winner?

Gail Devers.

Her time of 10.82 seconds was a personal best.

"This was a long time coming," she said on the victory podium, a gold medal hanging from her neck and flowers in her hands. "It means my Graves' disease is over. I'm back where I wanted to be, so it feels great."

Five days later, Gail was leading in the 100-meter hurdles when she caught her toe on the last barrier. She tripped, losing a chance at a second gold medal.

Gail took it in stride. After all, she had already made one of the greatest comebacks in track history.

10
CURT FLOOD
A Flood Tide

*B*atter up. It was, figuratively speaking, the bottom of the ninth as Curt Flood stepped up to the plate. Everything that Flood valued was on the line. What happened on this day could change the sports world forever.

As he entered the witness box, Flood glanced over at the heavy hitters on the other team. The commissioner of baseball and officials from every major league club were there. They wore stern expressions and glared at Flood. They were not pleased. Many of his own teammates were against him. In fact, a lot of people in the baseball world thought he was crazy.

In the hushed courtroom, Flood was sworn in to testify.

This powerful moment had drawn the widespread attention of the media and the interest of millions of sports fans.

Flood was challenging one of baseball's longstanding rules, a sports law that he felt to be unjust.

Unlike today's highly paid free agents, baseball players in the 1960s and earlier couldn't choose their teams. They were forced to be the property of a team for life. This policy was called the reserve clause. It was the opposite of free agency. A player then only had two choices: 1) he could stay with the same team and

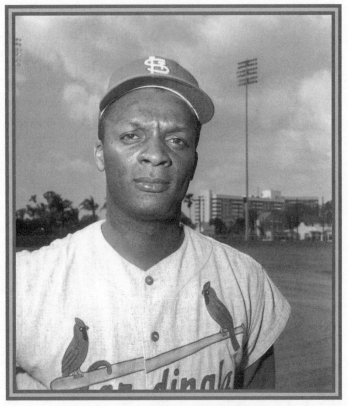

Curt Flood, outfielder for the St. Louis Cardinals, in 1965

accept whatever salary was offered until he was traded to another team or 2) he could leave baseball.

In the sixties, almost everything was changing in America— everything, it seemed, but baseball. There was social unrest in the country. The civil rights movement was in full force. Blacks were fighting for equal rights.

Since Jackie Robinson had broken baseball's color line in 1947, some measure of equality was evident in the sport. By the late fifties, there was a black player on every major league team. But in other types of reform, America's "national game" was lagging far behind the rest of the country.

Flood felt it was about time to make some improvements in the way baseball was being run. Baseball had become a big business, and many players felt that the people who held the power in the sport were taking advantage of them. Flood agreed. He was particularly upset about the reserve clause. He had decided to take on the entire baseball organization and now he was standing before the court.

He had to win this one, or he would lose everything. Could he do it, or would he strike out?

Born in Houston, Texas, in 1938, Curt Flood was the youngest of six children. When he was just a little boy, the family moved to Oakland, California. It wasn't an easy life. There was poverty and crime in Flood's neighborhood. Many kids got in trouble with the law, but Flood didn't have time for trouble. He was busy playing baseball.

At the age of nine, Flood joined the Police Athletic League and continued to polish his baseball skills. As a teenager, he played American Legion ball. He was small for his age—only 105 pounds—but he was a solid player. When he made the team at McClymonds High School, Flood faced several obstacles. His coaches recognized his talent, but they were worried. Flood was still much smaller than the other boys his age. Even though he played well, he was overshadowed by teammates Frank Robinson and Vada Pinson, who later went on to become big league stars.

Size wasn't the only problem confronting Flood. At that time a black player had to possess super ability to make the majors. Flood was good—but certainly not a power hitter like Robinson or Pinson.

People told Flood he would never make it in major league baseball.

Determined to prove them wrong, Flood set out to become a great all-around ballplayer. He started to work extra hard on his defense. Day after day, night after night, he practiced fielding ground balls and fly balls. His defense improved steadily.

It wasn't his excellent fielding, though, that attracted the interest of scouts. It was Flood's batting average—over .400—that caught their attention. He wasn't a slugger, but he had a sharp batting eye and he consistently made contact with the ball.

The scouts were impressed. Flood signed a contract with the Cincinnati Reds organization in 1956. They paid him $4,000 for the season and sent him to one of their farm teams in the Deep South: High Point–Thomasville of the Class B Carolina League. It was one of the lower minor leagues in the professional system.

Flood was ready and eager for the challenges of playing pro ball, but he wasn't prepared for the struggle that lay ahead. As the only black player on his team in the Carolina

League, Flood met with abuse from hostile fans. Racists in the stands called him terrible names. They even threatened him.

Showing remarkable courage, Flood answered the racial taunts the best way he knew how—with his bat, glove, and speed. And in spite of the difficult situation, Flood managed to play better than anyone else in the league. By the end of the 1956 season, he was named the Carolina League's player of the year.

Flood's hard work impressed the Reds. They called him up to the major leagues for a few games.

With so many successes, Flood felt he had earned a raise. After all, he was the Carolina League's player of the year. One day he walked into the office of the Reds' general manager to talk about his contract. Flood was shocked when the general manager refused his request for a raise. Again Flood would have to play for the same salary. He signed the contract for the 1957 season. He had no other choice.

Flood didn't get a raise, but did get a promotion. He moved up to a higher minor league with the Reds' farm club in Savannah, Georgia. Another great year, another late-season call-up to the Reds. Once again, Flood expected a raise. Instead, he got something totally unexpected—a trade to St. Louis.

He was upset, but it was baseball law. For as long as the sport had existed, players had been swapped from one team to another just like baseball cards. It was business. Flood was no exception. He joined the Cardinals.

Flood had just turned twenty when he was penciled in as the Cardinals' center fielder. Center field, one of the most important positions in baseball, is usually reserved for the best outfielder on the team. He has the quickest glove, strongest arm, and fastest feet. He covers more ground than any of the three outfielders. Flood did not disappoint. He made the Cardinals' center field position his own.

In 1966, Flood did something amazing. He played an entire major league season—160 games, 396 chances—without making an error. He also set a National League record for consecutive games without an error—226.

Just as important to the Cardinals were Flood's batting skills. The measuring stick for a top hitter is .300. Mostly a singles hitter, Flood batted over .300 six times in twelve seasons with the Cardinals. In one doubleheader, he tied a record with eight straight hits. In both 1963 and 1964, Flood was the only major leaguer with 200 hits for the season.

Flood was small for a major leaguer even then—he was only 5-foot-9 and 160 pounds—but his team could always rely on him to produce runs with his bat and base-running ability.

The 1960s were a golden age of Cardinals baseball. From 1964 to 1968, the Cardinals won three pennants and two world championships. In the center of their successes were Flood and a group of solid players. Through the sixties such outstanding players as Bob Gibson, Bill White, Orlando Cepeda, Roger Maris, Ken Boyer, and Lou Brock wore the

Curt Flood

Curt Flood practices with the Washington Senators in 1970.

Cardinals uniform. Flood was so highly regarded that he was made team captain from 1965 to 1969.

When the Cardinals failed to win the pennant in 1969, owner August A. Busch Jr. started to break up the team. One of the first to go was Flood, in a blockbuster trade with the Philadelphia Phillies.

Flood was shocked when he learned he had been traded

after twelve years in St. Louis. And traded to a top team? No. He was traded to the Phillies, then one of the worst teams in baseball. They played in an old stadium. The so-called "City of Brotherly Love" had been the scene of many racial incidents.

Flood was unhappy with the trade to the Phillies. He had been traded once before, from Cincinnati to St. Louis. He didn't want to be traded again.

On Christmas Eve 1969, Flood wrote a letter to Baseball Commissioner Bowie Kuhn asking for permission to bargain with other teams. The answer was no.

Kuhn was the highest authority in baseball. Flood had to find another way to change this baseball practice that he thought was so unfair. He felt that the reserve clause was not legal. He made a momentous decision: He would fight for his personal freedom by suing baseball. It would be one man against the baseball world. David against Goliath.

It was even more astonishing because Flood was being paid one of the highest salaries in the game. And the Phillies were going to give him a raise.

But Flood said no. To him the reserve clause was like slavery. In his lawsuit, he said players were "bought like cattle." It didn't matter to Flood that he would be paid $100,000.

"A well-paid slave is a slave nonetheless," Flood said.

He knew it would take a lot of courage and a lot of money, but he decided to go ahead with the lawsuit. Flood *vs.* American baseball. It would be tough. He convinced the Players Association to help him. But the Association didn't have enough money for a good lawyer.

Flood found a lawyer who would work just for expenses. His name: Arthur J. Goldberg, former Supreme Court justice. He was one of the most famous lawyers in the country. Goldberg decided to take the case without salary because he believed in Flood's cause.

Curt Flood had been one of the most popular players in baseball. As soon as he went public with his suit against baseball, he was not so popular anymore. Instead of being famous, Flood became infamous. He lost his money. He lost many of his fans. He lost his chance to go to the Hall of Fame.

Owners, fans—even fellow players—thought Flood's case was ridiculous. Some thought he was just looking for more money. Others felt Flood was making a stand for the black movement. The press called him a revolutionary; some people predicted that he was out to destroy America's favorite pastime. Owners expressed fear that the end of the reserve clause would be the end of baseball.

Flood received hate mail and death threats. One of the letters compared him to Benedict Arnold, the American Revolutionary War traitor.

Flood admitted that he had trouble sleeping. "I've had second thoughts about my suit," he said. "But I think I'm on the right track." He added: "I'm not trying to create chaos or end baseball. I just want to stand up like a human being."

On May 19, 1970, Flood walked into the federal court-house in lower Manhattan to take on major league baseball. The odds looked overwhelming.

What chance of success did one baseball player have against Baseball Commissioner Kuhn, the presidents of the National and American Leagues, and the chief executives of all the twenty-four clubs?

During the trial not one of Flood's fellow players had the courage to testify against the reserve clause. But two Hall of Famers—Jackie Robinson and Hank Greenberg—took the stand to speak against the unfair practice. Jim Brosnan, an ex-pitcher and celebrated author, also testified in support of Flood's case.

The trial took many weeks. On the stand Flood repeated his demand for the right to approve or disapprove when the decision was made to trade him to another team. A lawyer asked him which team he would like to play for.

"The team that makes me the best offer," replied the thirty-two-year-old outfielder.

Finally, Judge Irving Ben Cooper made his decision.

He said "reasonable men" could find a solution outside of court. He ruled against Flood.

Strike one!

Flood appealed. The United States Second Circuit Court of Appeals upheld the lower court's decision.

Strike two!

Flood took his battle to the highest judicial authority in

the U.S.—the Supreme Court. By this time Flood had sat out the entire 1970 season.

While the case was waiting to come before the Supreme Court justices, Flood considered returning to baseball. Flood was assured that he could play without hurting his lawsuit. In 1971, he signed with the Washington Senators. When he got out on the field, however, he just didn't measure up to the player he once was. He was unhappy with his performance. Had he been away from the game too long? After just thirteen games he quit with only a .200 batting average.

Finally, the Supreme Court handed down its decision in 1972. The justices upheld the rulings of the two lower courts.

Strike three!

Flood was out.

Out, but not forgotten…

Although he had lost his suit, Flood's courageous stand had made a dramatic impact on baseball. A lot of people had read or heard about his court case and it had started them thinking. Baseball hadn't made any significant changes since Jackie Robinson had broken the color barrier in 1947. Maybe it was time for the sport to dust off the cobwebs on another very old concept.

Four years after Flood had brought national attention to the unfairness of the reserve clause, an arbitrator granted free agency to pitchers Andy Messersmith and Dave

McNally. From then on, a player would only be bound to a team for the length of his contract.

The reserve clause was dead. Curt Flood had paved the way to a new era in baseball.

Players were now able to make deals on their own. Once their contracts were fulfilled with one team, they could sign with anyone they wished. They were known as "free agents." Before Flood died in 1997 at the age of 59, he was able to see the impact he had made on baseball. Players were making millions of dollars and in some cases were able to control where they could be traded.

"Every major league baseball player owed a debt to Curt Flood that can never be repaid," player representatives David Cone of the American League and Tom Glavine of the National League said in a joint statement at the time of Flood's death.

"With the odds against him," they said, "Flood had the courage to take a stand for what he knew was right."

11
ROCKY BLEIER
Man on a Mission

*O*n a hot August Vietnamese night in 1969, Rocky Bleier paused for a moment, shifting the heavy grenade launcher to ease his aching arms. His platoon was on a search patrol among the rice paddies in a valley called Diep Duc.

A figure appeared from the shadows, his hands raised high over his head in a position of surrender. The man told the American soldiers that he was tired of the war and wanted to give himself up. He said there were more Viet Cong like him, and he offered to lead the Americans to them. Bleier and the rest of his platoon followed slowly, cautiously.

Suddenly the man darted into the rice paddies. A burst of machine-gun fire tore through the darkness.

Ambush! *someone screamed.*

The Americans hit the ground.

"I saw a fluttering of leaves where the machine gun was. I raised myself on my side to fire my rifle grenade, when a guy behind me yelled 'Rocky' and at the same time I felt a thud in my left thigh," Bleier said.

One of the machine-gun bullets had found Bleier's leg.

Lying on his back, Bleier kept firing until he was out of ammunition. Then he crawled back to the other soldiers. Together they retreated through the jungle back to the command post. They did not know that the Viet Cong were following close behind them.

The Americans stopped to give Captain Tom Murphy a chance to contact the command post. Bleier was sitting about six feet away when he heard something hit the ground.

"Grenade!" Murphy yelled.

Bleier rolled away and the force of the explosion knocked him unconscious.

"When I woke, I saw a hole two feet deep where I had been sitting," Bleier said.

Then another grenade struck the captain in the middle of the back and bounced toward Bleier. Should I jump back with the grenade rolling after me, he wondered, or jump over it? He didn't have much time to make a choice.

Bleier jumped forward, and the grenade went off.

"It caught the captain between the knees," Bleier recalled. "I got it in the right foot."

Reinforcements finally arrived. They carried Bleier to a helicopter and flew him to an aid station. At some point the wounded soldier lost consciousness.

When he came to the next morning, an American doctor was working on his legs, painstakingly removing shrapnel piece by piece. The doctor looked up for a minute and stared at his patient's face.

"Rocky Bleier?" the doctor asked in amazement. "Notre Dame captain?"

Bleier nodded.

Rocky Bleier

The doctor introduced himself with a sly grin. "I'm from USC. I was at that game you beat us 51–0."

This is ironic, Bleier thought. A doctor from Southern Cal, Notre Dame's biggest rival, was operating on him.

Then the horror of the situation hit Bleier. Would he ever be able to play football again? "Oh, no!" Bleier screamed, shutting his eyes in dismay.

When he was born in Appleton, Wisconsin, in 1946, his parents named him Robert Patrick Bleier. But that name didn't stick.

"My dad owned a bar in Appleton and we lived above it," Bleier remembered. "When I was born and the guys in the bar asked him how I was, he told them, 'He's like a little rock.' Then they'd come in after that and ask him, 'How's the little rock?'"

So Mr. Bleier nicknamed his son "Rocky." The name turned out to be a good one. It suited Bleier's toughness of character in sports and he carried it through every time he stepped on a football field.

Like most every other sports-minded boy in Appleton, Rocky Bleier grew up with dreams of being a professional football player. With the Green Bay Packers the dominant pro team in the state, just about all of Wisconsin was football crazy. Green Bay, located in northeastern Wisconsin on the shores of the Fox River, was a short drive from Bleier's house.

Bleier loved football, but he loved other sports, too. At

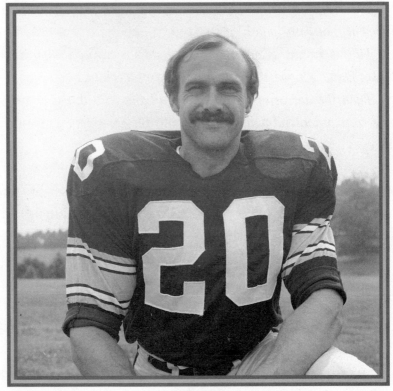

Rocky Bleier

Appleton Xavier High School, he was one of the best all-around athletes in school history. He not only starred on the football team but he also played basketball and baseball and competed on the track team.

The young athlete learned early to set goals for himself and to work hard until he reached them. In high school, his first goal was to make the football team. With that mission accomplished, his next goal was to help Appleton Xavier win the state championship. Under his leadership, Rocky's high school football squad went on to become the top team in Wisconsin.

Rocky's next goal: a national championship in college.

Bleier played three seasons with the Notre Dame Fighting Irish, one of the most famous football teams in America, and captained them as a senior. Once again he led his team to a championship.

Still, he was not regarded as a top choice for any of the National Football League (NFL) teams. He waited through sixteen rounds of the 1968 NFL draft and watched while 416 other college players were picked. Finally Bleier was selected by the Pittsburgh Steelers.

Although he was picked low in the draft, Bleier aimed high again. He set out to make his mark as a starting running back for the Steelers.

But that goal would have to wait. As a rookie Bleier was mostly a "special teams" player. One of his main jobs was to play on the kickoff teams, a role that required a passionate spirit and a high threshold of pain.

Fans and teammates loved Bleier's enthusiasm. They roared their approval when No. 20 charged into the battle headfirst, putting his body at risk without worry of injury.

Teammates admired Bleier's eagerness, but they valued him even more for his dependability. He was one of the hardest working players on the team.

In 1968, a war was raging in Vietnam. With only two games left in the 1968 season, Bleier received his draft notice from the U.S. Army. His football career would have to be put on hold. Bleier prepared to go to Vietnam with the idea of "serving my time and not getting hurt."

Rocky didn't know much about the war—except that it had become more and more unpopular in the United States. He knew even less about the country he was heading toward, but he would soon learn more than he ever wanted to know about that faraway place the other soldiers called "Nam."

For months Rocky did his duty alongside his fellow soldiers in the steamy rice fields, dreaming of the time when he could return to the football fields back home. Then came the ambush that left him severely wounded in both legs.

At first, the doctor from Southern Cal feared that he might have to amputate one of Rocky's feet. He succeeded in saving Rocky's foot—and his life—but chances for a complete recovery looked slim. Bleier was later flown to hospitals in Da Nang, the Philippines, Tokyo, and finally, Fort Riley in Kansas. He underwent several operations. He lost so much weight that he looked like a different person. "I had gone from 210 pounds to 165," he later remembered.

His medical advisers told him that he might be able to walk normally again. But play football? Impossible.

It seemed his football career had ended before it really got started.

Bleier had other ideas.

"I wanted to play pro football and I thought I could," Bleier said.

While recovering in the Fort Riley hospital, Bleier notified Steelers owner Art Rooney that he was ready to resume his football career. Rooney invited Bleier back—perhaps partly out of sympathy. Rooney would have had to be wildly optimistic to expect that after such serious injuries Bleier would ever make it in the NFL. That had to be the thinking of the players as well.

"When I rejoined the team in 1970," Bleier remembered, "the players were all great, but I had the obvious feeling it was pity."

Could Bleier overcome his serious injuries and perform as an NFL running back again? It seemed unlikely.

But he was determined to try.

He began working out, even though he didn't have full feeling in his right foot.

"The first time I ran was only for a half mile and it was very difficult," Bleier recalled. "The foot hurt. It was like running with a stone in your shoe. I couldn't catch my breath."

Then he joined the Steelers in training camp.

"I guess I did have some doubts deep inside," Bleier said. "When I first started working out in the spring of 1970, boy, I knew I had a long way to go. It was going to be a tough struggle, in that I didn't have the speed."

Worse yet, Bleier was still suffering the aftereffects of the war injuries. And a hamstring pull further complicated matters.

"I was limping and couldn't perform well," Bleier said.

The Steelers put Bleier on the injured reserve list. That bought him another year to get in better shape. The next season they placed him on the Taxi Squad, a non-playing reserve unit that is a part of all NFL teams. That kept him alive on the Steelers' roster for one more year.

In 1972, after another operation, Bleier's recovery was just about complete. He still needed to wear a special shoe on his right foot, and he could only run on half the foot. But he felt ready. The Steelers reactivated Bleier, putting him back on the special teams unit.

Offensive coach Dick Hoak said Bleier was the best special teams player the Steelers had. And he was still the hardest worker.

"When he came back, he weighed only 165 pounds," Hoak said, "but he started lifting weights and soon got back to his playing weight of 210 pounds."

Bleier had still not reached his cherished goal as a starting running back, though.

"I was the fifth or sixth running back on the team and I did not play much," Bleier said. "My only contribution was to the special teams and I got depressed. I felt they weren't using me; they didn't have confidence in me. I didn't want to be a special teams player all my life. I thought maybe I should retire."

After speaking to a priest who was a family friend, Bleier decided to stick it out a little while longer. In 1974, Bleier did get into the backfield. But he only served as a blocker for star running back Franco Harris.

Then before the fifth game of the year, two of the

Steelers' higher rated running backs were injured. Coach Chuck Noll put Bleier into the lineup alongside Harris. In his first start as a running back, Bleier rushed for an impressive 78 yards.

Bleier showed he was able to start. But would he be able to star?

In 1975, Bleier was in the lineup against the Green Bay Packers. He was playing against his home-state team, the team he used to root for growing up in Appleton.

Bleier especially wanted to put on a good show that day. And what a show it was!

Pittsburgh Steeler Rocky Bleier runs with the ball.

He carried the ball thirty-five times and rushed for a career-high 163 yards as the Steelers beat the Packers 16–13. It would be Bleier's best day in pro football, and a day he would remember for the rest of his career.

"Someone of my caliber doesn't get that kind of a day very often," Bleier said modestly, "and it was a game that was played back in Milwaukee, kind of in front of the home-town crowd."

With Bleier playing a key role, the Steelers went on to win the Super Bowl title that year. He also contributed to the Steelers' three other Super Bowl victories in the 1970s, but that first Super Bowl win was always the most important to Bleier.

As he nervously stood in the runway waiting to be introduced along with his teammates at Super Bowl IX in 1975, many thoughts went through Bleier's mind.

"I was thinking about all the great teams that had played before us in the Super Bowl," he said, "and just thinking here was a little kid from Appleton, Wisconsin, who is able to participate in one as a starting running back."

Bleier had always been goal oriented. After a long and torturous journey to Vietnam and back, after so many operations and the long struggle to regain his strength, Bleier had reached his final goals: to be a starting running back in the NFL and to win a Super Bowl.

And he had achieved his aims through sheer determination and hard work. The little "rock" had more than lived up to his name.

12
EKATERINA GORDEEVA
Skating for Sergei

Katia Gordeeva was terrified. Although she had won two Olympic gold medals and four world championships in figure skating, this was the hardest thing she'd ever had to do.

But it was something she must do.

As she waited to go out on the ice, she knew that she was not skating for herself, she was skating for Sergei. Her beloved Sergei. She simply could not fail.

During a practice session just three months earlier, her husband and longtime skating partner, Sergei Grinkov, had suddenly collapsed and died of a heart attack. He was only twenty-eight.

Katia was devastated. How could she go on without him?

Although figure skating is highly competitive, in times of trouble the ice skating community bands together and becomes one big family. Dozens of friends rallied to her side.

The skaters grieved with Katia for their fallen comrade. They put their talents together to honor Sergei with a special benefit performance. Proceeds from the tribute, called "A Celebration of a Life," would go to a fund for Katia and her three-year-old daughter, Daria. A sold-out crowd of 15,000 jammed the Hartford

PROFILES IN SPORTS COURAGE

Olympic gold medal skater Ekaterina Gordeeva

(Connecticut) Civic Center on February 27, 1996, to watch the all-star show.

Katia Gordeeva would be making her first public appearance on the ice since the loss of her husband. The Russian couple had been brilliant international stars in the pairs competition for many years. But now for the first time in her life, Katia would be skating publicly as a solo performer.

She knew the tribute to Sergei was something that she simply had to do.

"You can't lock yourself inside or you'll die," Katia said. "My mother told me, 'You have to get up now. You have a daughter to live for.'"

Katia had planned her routine as a personal tribute to her late husband. She wanted everything to go perfectly.

Could she do it in her emotional state? Her heart was still heavy with sorrow.

Charged with emotion, she was ready to give the performance of her life. She couldn't help thinking about how Sergei had always comforted her before they went out on the ice together. This time, there was no Sergei to do that.

She felt all alone, terribly alone.

The crowd waited expectantly for her to step into the spotlight...

Her given name was Ekaterina, but friends called her "Katia." Skating came naturally to her while growing up in Moscow. Her father Alexander Gordeeva was a member of a Russian military dance group. Katia couldn't remember a day when she wasn't doing something that involved her skating.

Sergei Grinkov was a natural skater, too. At the age of five he was already preparing for a skating trial at the Central Army Sports Club School. A government-sponsored program was looking for the Soviets' next Olympic stars. Sergei soon found that he enjoyed skating better than schoolwork. By the time he was fourteen, he was bigger and better than most of his fellow skaters.

Sergei's instructors were impressed with his talent. They thought, however, that he would do better in pairs than as a singles skater. They teamed him with Katia, a ten-year-old ponytailed pixie he had met several years before at a Moscow skating club.

At first Sergei was reluctant to skate with Katia. He was full of good humor, always telling jokes. He didn't know what to make of this stern-faced little girl who hardly ever smiled.

"I could never lift this girl," Sergei complained to his coach.

Katia didn't like the arrangement any better than Sergei did. The two young skaters did have one important thing in common, though: they were both deeply dedicated to their sport. Day after day they came to the rink and practiced together. Soon they began feeling more comfortable with each other.

Pairs skating demands a great deal from the performers. In some ways it is more challenging than singles skating. There must be a sensitive connection between partners. The two skaters need to trust each other completely and without question. The complicated moves they perform together require delicate precision. Just one wrong move or a split-second mistake in timing during a lift or a double axel throw can result in a terrible, career-ending injury. Katia Gordeeva's life was literally in her partner's hands when Sergei tossed her up in the air and she made several dizzying revolutions.

As they spent more and more time at the rink, the trust between Katia and Sergei grew stronger. They liked each other. And they both loved to work.

They bonded as if they were brother and sister.

Katia and Sergei couldn't stay away from the rink, and they couldn't tear themselves away when it was time to leave practice sessions.

On the ice, they looked like a mismatched pair. She was so small, just about 5 feet tall and less than 100 pounds. He stood a good 10 inches taller and weighed 180 pounds.

But they were a perfect team. Their difference in size actually worked to their advantage: they developed moves that were both athletic and artistic.

The skater who had told his coach that he "could never lift this girl" was now lifting her with ease and grace. One writer said that Grinkov held Gordeeva aloft and set her down as if she were a small bird.

Their overhead moves were so quiet and smooth that if you closed your eyes, you could hardly tell they were in the arena. The couple's signature move: a quadruple twist in which Sergei threw Katia high in the air, allowing her to make four revolutions before landing gracefully in his arms.

"Sergei was strong," recalled Vladimir Zakharov, who became the pair's trainer in 1982. "I would tell them, 'That's enough for today.' But they would want to practice until the night. It was their goal to get to the top."

Their hard work paid off. In 1986, they won the world championship. Katia was only fourteen years old, still the "younger sister" to Sergei's more mature eighteen.

Two years later, the pair captured the gold medal at the Calgary Olympics.

Then something happened that neither of them had ever expected. The affection they had for each other blossomed into love.

One day, Sergei confided to his sister Natasha, "Katia has become so beautiful!"

It was the beginning of a true love story.

Fellow skaters marveled at the couple's devotion to each other. "Their eyes never left each other during the whole performance," said American skater Paul Wylie. "No one else does that in pairs skating. It can be very distracting, looking into someone else's eyes while you're skating, but it never was for them. It was natural."

After winning their fourth world championship in 1990, Sergei and Katia turned professional. They married in 1991 and one year later, two events brought the newlyweds much happiness.

First, Katia gave birth to a baby girl. The couple named her Daria. Second, there was a change in the rules after the 1992 Olympic Games in Albertville, France. Professionals were now allowed to compete in the Olympics.

Four weeks after giving birth, Katia was back on the ice with her husband, preparing for the 1994 Games to be held in Lillehammer, Norway. Both were thrilled.

"We wanted to show people how we have changed," Katia said.

Skating experts predicted one of the greatest Olympic pairs competitions in history. Katia and Sergei weren't the only previous gold medal winners from Russia in that event at the '94 Games. They faced a serious challenge from Natalia Mishkutienok and Artur Dmitriev, who had won the gold two years earlier at Albertville.

Before Katia and Sergei took the ice, they had to wait for Mishkutienok and Dmitriev to perform. Katia and Sergei could hear the wild cheers of the audience as their opponents went through a physically demanding and theatrical four-and-a-half minute routine.

Then it was Katia and Sergei's turn. Katia was especially nervous. It would be difficult to follow such a dramatic performance.

"Everyone was waiting for us to do something special," she said. "We felt this, too."

The music of Beethoven's "Moonlight Sonata" filled the arena as Katia and Sergei went into their elegant, more restrained routine. The audience sat perfectly still, mesmerized by the graceful couple.

Their performance was not seamless. Twice Sergei faltered slightly during the routine. But no one seemed to mind that he was not as picture-perfect as he had been in the past.

The judges awarded the pair the gold medal, their second in the Olympics.

Katia found this win even more satisfying than the first one. "I was sixteen and everything was too easy for me," she said of the first time she and Sergei won the gold. "The last Olympics was another life. Now I try to remember each face, each person. I try to take in everything."

The couple returned to the pro circuit and settled into a home in the United States, in Simsbury, Connecticut. Soon, other skaters from the former Soviet Union joined their little community, including gold medal winner Oksana Baiul. Katia and Sergei felt lucky to have so many dear friends nearby.

They had family close to them, too. Katia's mother came over from Russia to take care of little Daria when the couple was on tour. Katia was happy. Everything seemed perfect.

Then her world came crashing down.

It was a normal day. Katia and her husband were practicing a routine at Lake Placid, New York, preparing a program for the "Stars on Ice" tour featuring some of the world's greatest skaters. Suddenly Sergei slipped out of her arms and collapsed on the ice. A short while later, he was gone. He had suffered a heart attack while doing what he loved most.

Katia was overcome with grief. Left without her beloved Sergei, her main support, she felt she couldn't go on. How could she survive a tragedy like that? It was difficult. When sad thoughts threatened to overwhelm her, Katia would put on her skates and go out on the ice.

"If I skate, then I feel better and I feel more comfortable," she said. "I just feel like I have to skate."

When the ice skating world honored her husband with an all-star show three months after his death, Katia was ready to go back on the ice.

Ekaterina Gordeeva skates a tribute for her husband Sergei Grinkov in 1996.

"A Celebration of a Life" featured such international stars as Baiul, Brian Boitano, Kristi Yamaguchi, and Scott Hamilton.

As the other skaters went through the opening processional number, Katia waited behind the curtain for her entrance. She was too nervous to watch them. The music of "Moonlight Sonata" filled the air, and brought back memories of her performances with Sergei. It was one of their favorite musical pieces. It was almost unbearable for Katia.

Finally, it was her turn to go out on the ice. The crowd stood and gave her a roaring ovation as she skated out.

Then the audience settled back in silence to watch Katia's powerful and sensitive tribute to her late husband. As she skated to Mahler's Symphony no. 5, no words were necessary to know the deep sorrow that Katia was feeling. Her movements on the ice told the whole story and revealed her most personal feelings in a re-enactment of her tragedy:

She searches the crowd. Sergei is nowhere to be found. In despair, she buries her head in her hands. She glides to her knees and kisses the ice. She holds her arms up to the heavens. She mourns a lost love ...

When she finished the program, Katia walked off the ice with her hands extended, as if still searching for Sergei. The arena rocked with cheers. Katia broke into tears as she came back to take her bows.

"I don't think any of us can fathom the amount of strength and courage it took for Katia to come out tonight and share her soul with all of us," Hamilton said.

The pain of losing Sergei eventually eased, and Katia was able to summon the courage to go back to work. She toured with her friends in the famed "Stars on Ice" show. Little by little she gained back her energy, both emotional and physical. In 1996, she told her story in a best-selling book, *My Sergei: A Love Story.*

In 2002, she married Ilia Kulik, an Olympic skater she had met on tour in 1998. They have a daughter, Elizaveta. "I'm trying," Katia said, "to live more for the kids."

Katia was no longer terrified. Although Sergei would always be in her heart, that part of her life was over.

She had already faced the hardest part of her battle. Just as she had found the courage to honor her husband in the "Celebration of a Life" show, deep within herself she had also found the courage to go on.

CONCLUSION

What is true courage? Is it the dedication to principles Junius Kellogg portrayed when he turned down easy money to throw the game? Kerri Strug's gritty determination to try one more jump, despite a broken ankle? Muhammad Ali's resolution to risk his career and even jail time to protect his religious freedom? As we have seen in the stories of these remarkable men and women of sports, courage can take many forms.

All of the athletes in this book faced a seemingly final "no." Others told them that they would never make the major leagues playing with only one hand, that they would never play football again after suffering a terrible war injury, that they could never overcome the barriers confronting them. But all of them found within themselves their own brand of courage to triumph over the "no," to push past intense opposition or physical hardship, and to realize their dreams.

BIBLIOGRAPHICAL NOTE

When I was the college basketball writer for The Associated Press, I sat down for an interview with Ken Norton, onetime basketball coach at Manhattan College. In very fine detail, Norton related a great adventure in his life: the courageous story of Junius Kellogg and his part in uncovering one of the biggest gambling scandals in college basketball history. That exclusive interview was the basis for one of the chapters in this book, "Blowing The Whistle."

I also had the good fortune to interview Rocky Bleier during my time with The Associated Press. Bleier's recollections of his own great adventure provided the material for another story in this book, "Man on a Mission."

In addition to personal interviews, I used a number of newspaper and magazine articles to research the stories in this book: The Associated Press, *Sports Illustrated*, *Sports Illustrated for Kids*, *New York Times*, *Newsweek*, *Los Angeles Times*, *The Times* (United Kingdom), *People*, *USA Today*, and *The Washington Post*.

I also found helpful the Current Biography Yearbook

ABOUT THE AUTHOR

Longtime sports writer **Ken Rappoport** is the author of dozens of books for young readers and adults, including *Ladies First: Women Athletes Who Made a Difference*, also with Peachtree Publishers. Ken has written about the NCAA basketball championship, minor league baseball, college football rivalries, and numerous teams and their players. He received a national award from *Writer's Digest* for a profile on St. John's University basketball coach Lou Carnesecca and has contributed to *The Saturday Evening Post* and *USA Today*. At The Associated Press, Rappoport covered every major sport out of New York for thirty years and was the AP's national hockey writer for fourteen years. He covered the World Series, NCAA Finals, Olympics, and Stanley Cup playoffs, among other events.

Ken lives in New Jersey.

series available in most libraries as well as some of the leading Internet sites.

If you want to learn more about these athletes, you may find the following books of interest:

Fighting Back, by Rocky Bleier with Terry O'Neil

Gail Devers (Overcoming Adversity), by Richard Worth

The Greatest: My Own Story, by Muhammad Ali with Richard Durham

Great Time Coming, by David Falkner

It's Not About the Bike: My Journey Back to Life, by Lance Armstrong with Sally Jenkins

Janet Guthrie: A Life at Full Thottle, by Janet Guthrie

Jim Abbott: Against the Odds, by Ellen Emerson White

Landing on my Feet: A Diary of Dreams, by Kerri Strug with John Lopez

My Sergei: A Love Story, by Ekaterina Gordeeva with E. M. Swift

Scandals of '51: How the Gamblers Almost Killed College Basketball, by Charles Rosen

The Way It Is, by Curt Flood

Women Explorers of the Mountains, by Margo McLoone and Kathryn Besio